# Using Picture Books to Promote Empathy, Belonging, and Social Justice in Pre-K and Kindergarten

# Using Picture Books to Promote Empathy, Belonging, and Social Justice in Pre-K and Kindergarten

Isauro M. Escamilla, Iliana Alanís, and Daniel Meier

Foreword by Fabienne Doucet

Teachers College Press

Teachers College, Columbia University

Published by Teachers College Press,® 1234 Amsterdam Avenue, New York, NY 10027

Copyright © 2026 by Teachers College, Columbia University

Front cover design by Holly Grundon / BHG Graphics. Photo by monkeybusinessimages / iStock by Getty Images.

*Library of Congress Cataloging-in-Publication Data is available at loc.gov*

ISBN 978-0-8077-8395-5 (paper)
ISBN 978-0-8077-8353-5 (hardcover)
ISBN 978-0-8077-8396-2 (ebook)

Printed on acid-free paper
Manufactured in the United States of America

*We dedicate this book to all educators who recognize the significance of promoting equity and social justice in early childhood contexts. We hope this text will contribute to enacting meaningful child-centered discussions that affirm and support children's lived experiences, multilingualism, and multiliteracies. We also dedicate this book to Dr. Patricia Sullivan, who tragically passed away a few months after she wrote her wonderful chapter for this book. Dr. Sullivan was a fierce advocate for early childhood education and the power of books to change children's lives.*

# Contents

# Foreword

I love everything about picture books, from the way they distill huge ideas into a few hundred words, to the imagination they foster for solving complicated problems, to the exquisite art they put in children's hands, to their magical ability to charm us every time we read them, even after hundreds of story times. Still, I surprised myself the first time I was compelled—literally in the middle of the night—to put to paper a phrase that played on a loop in my mind and that would become my first attempt at writing a picture book myself. It would take another 10 years for my bilingual picture book, *Love is Still Winning/El Amor Siempre Triunfa* (Doucet, 2024), which is about how love is made manifest in a community through everyday actions, to come into the world. It represents a beautiful union of my scholarly work as an early childhood teacher educator with my creative undertakings and underscores my excitement for Escamilla, Alanís, and Meier's new book, *Using Picture Books to Promote Empathy, Belonging, and Social Justice in Pre-K and Kindergarten*. My dual lens gives me unique insight into both the craft of creating meaningful children's literature and the classroom realities teachers face. My work preparing emerging educators has made clear teachers' need for resources that reflect their students' diverse experiences, and my picture book writing has taught me about the careful intentionality required to address complex topics for young audiences. The work Escamilla, Alanís, and Meier offer us in this book bridges that gap beautifully, providing both the theoretical foundation and practical tools that educators desperately need.

I first brought picture books into my practice as a teacher educator in 2009 when teaching a course on multicultural social studies for young children. The textbook I had chosen (Seefeldt & Galper, 2006) included at the end of every chapter a list of picture books related to its theme (e.g., "Happy to be Me," "Different Kinds of Families," "Wants and Needs"). A lifelong lover of picture books, I was thrilled to bring them to class and think with my students about how to use them as starting points for engaging in discussions about layered and complex topics like racism, inequality, and social justice, but my strategies were limited. *Using Picture Books to Promote Empathy, Belonging, and Social Justice in Pre-K and*

*Kindergarten* is the resource I never knew I needed! This book could not come at a better time. Since 2021, a movement to ban books has steadily and relentlessly pushed into schools, classrooms, and libraries, fueled by fear and hatred, with advocates determined to empty bookshelves of stories that tell the truth about U.S. history and celebrate the range of human experience (Meehan et al., 2024). Yet decades of research support the function of books as "mirrors, windows, and sliding glass doors" (Bishop, 1990) with which children can begin to understand the world around them, their place in it, and their power to change it.

Escamilla, Alanís, and Meier's important book unapologetically celebrates principles of social justice, equity, inclusion, love, and freedom while offering theoretically grounded, evidence-based tools and recommendations for how picture books can be leveraged to counter bias, discrimination, racism, and exclusion, and address the harmful effects of inequitable practices. *Using Picture Books to Promote Empathy, Belonging, and Social Justice in Pre-K and Kindergarten* arms educators with theoretical understanding, practical applications, a comprehensive approach to multilingualism, and strategies for centering the families and communities whose children populate their classrooms. It is accessible and appropriate for teachers from the newest novice to the most experienced. Furthermore, the resources it offers will have readers returning to it again and again as they continue to hone their practice in using picture books for building children's literacy skills, unpacking the richness of human experience, and reinforcing principles of equity and justice. While each chapter offers unique perspectives, core themes thread throughout the book to create a cohesive manual that fills an important gap in the field by demonstrating the multiple levels at which picture books can operate simultaneously in an educator's toolbox. These themes include affirming children's identities; emphasizing discussion and dialogue; valuing multilingualism and multiliteracies; engaging families as partners; and observing, documenting, and assessing children's understanding and growth.

As dominant systems and structures seek to ban books, ban words that tell the truth about the human experience, and ban ideas that would dare challenge the status quo, this book stands as a courageous counternarrative. By adopting the concepts and methods it presents and sharing its wisdom, educators and teacher educators will transform classrooms and communities into thoughtful, just spaces of possibility where love will continue to win.

—Fabienne Doucet
Executive Director
NYU Metropolitan Center for Research on
Equity and the Transformation of Schools

Professor of Early Childhood Education and Urban Education
Department of Teaching and Learning,
NYU Steinhardt School of Culture, Education, and Human Development
New York City, May 2025

## REFERENCES

Bishop, R. S. (1990). Mirrors, windows, and sliding glass doors. *Perspectives—Gerontological Nursing Association, 6*(3), ix–xi.

Doucet, F. (2024). *Love is still winning/El amor siempre triunfa* (J. de la Vega, Illus.). Lil' Libros.

Meehan, K., Baêta, S., Magnusson, T., & Markham, M. (2024). *Banned in the USA: Beyond the shelves.* PEN America. https://pen.org/report/beyond-the-shelves

Seefeldt, C., & Galper, A. (2006). *Active experiences for active children* (2nd ed.). Pearson Education.

# Using Picture Books
# to Promote Empathy,
# Belonging, and Social Justice
# in Pre-K and Kindergarten

# Introduction

As the world becomes increasingly complex, education and schools must play new roles in helping young children understand and apply new ideas to make the world a better place for all children, families, and educators. From racial violence to climate change to economic disparities to environmental injustices, young children need our guidance and wisdom to navigate new ideas and solutions to address these challenges. In addressing relevant theory and effective instructional practices, this book highlights six leading questions that preschool, transitional kindergarten, and kindergarten educators can consider when linking children's picture books with social justice and equity:

1. What are effective ways to research and select picture books with engaging and meaningful social justice and equity text and images that can validate and support children's life experiences and interests?
2. How can educators use picture books for social justice and equity in English-medium, informal multilingual, and dual language learning and immersion programs?
3. How can educators integrate children's picture books to support emergent and play-based language and literacy curricula?
4. How can picture books with social justice and equity content be used in theme-based language and literacy contexts?
5. How can educators complement their mandated language arts curriculum and assessments with the inclusion of picture books focused on social justice and equity?
6. To what extent can social justice and equity picture books support children, families, and educators as agentic actors for social and educational change?

In this book, the authors and contributors argue that schools, educators, and families can use children's picture books to support young children's awareness and application of principles of social justice, equity, inclusion, love, and freedom. As the authors, we argue that young children—those we meet and work with in preschool, transitional kindergarten, and kindergarten, in private schools, public schools, family childcare settings, and community programs—are at the pivotal age for building a foundational awareness of social justice and equity.

### Key Definition: Transitional Kindergarten

Transitional kindergarten currently exists in public schools in four states (California, Washington, Michigan, and Florida) and serves as a transition between preschool and kindergarten. For instance, in California, for the 2025–2026 school year, children who are 4 years old by September 1, 2025, can enter transitional kindergarten.

As experienced teachers of young children and as veteran early childhood teacher educators, we are also aware that crafting developmentally, culturally, and linguistically supportive and inclusive curriculum and teaching practices around children's picture books is a complicated endeavor. The process is a lifelong political, social, and educational journey, and one that necessitates a deep awareness of our own biases, myths, and stereotypes about human difference and identity in our schools and in our society. We also acknowledge that we are at a new crossroads in our society in terms of racial, political, and economic divisions, and must look for new ways forward to promote healthy dialogue, trust, and collaboration toward a mutually beneficial future. Children's picture books, we argue, are a profound vehicle for addressing social and historical issues and challenges and for providing young children with the ideas, dispositions, and problem-solving skills they will need as the future generation of leaders and community members.

This book also seeks to disrupt normative paradigms in language and literacy education that marginalize and exclude culturally and linguistically diverse children from accessing high-quality picture books that speak to children's talents, interests, experiences, and aspirations. As the authors and contributors of this book, we believe that picture books about social justice and equity play crucial roles in shaping the hearts, minds, and bodies of all young children by promoting a more inclusive and equitable society. Introducing developmentally appropriate and child responsive social justice concepts at an early age helps children to develop a deeper understanding of their worlds and to value different cultures, races, and languages. Through critical discussions and engagement with picture books, children can develop important foundational social values of inclusion and respect, nascent identities as agentic actors in the world, and principles of civic and democratic engagement.

In selecting and engaging with meaningful picture books with social justice and equity content, images, and authorship, classroom teachers and teacher educators can address equity pedagogy to challenge the realities of racism in their classrooms, and to examine their own exposure to and contribution to racism and discrimination (Husband, 2012; Singleton & Linton, 2006). Antibias education (Derman-Sparks & Edwards, 2010; Iruka et al., 2022) supports children and their families as they develop a sense of identity and fairness and advocate for the rights of others. Educators learn to go beyond a colorblind curriculum and become sufficiently knowledgeable and empowered to address social justice issues and the harmful effects of inequitable practices (Kuh et al., 2016; Sturdivant & Alanís, 2019).

Ample research has shown that young children are aware of the manifestations and effects of social inequities and racism at an early age (Ramsey, 2004; Tatum, 2021). Young children develop racial awareness starting as early as three months (Quinn et al., 2016) and can display clear racial preferences by preschool (MacNevin & Berman, 2017). By 3 and 4 years of age, young children notice and talk about race and are capable of revealing their understandings about social justice issues through drawings, play, and discourse (Tatum, 2017).

Research has also shown that children of color who identify less with their racial backgrounds do less well academically and feel the impacts of inequity more than their white peers (Zirkel & Johnson, 2016). Positive identity development can lead to positive impacts on children's educational attitudes and learning (Carson, 2009) as well as on their overall emotional well-being (Brittian et al., 2013; Whittaker & Neville, 2010). As schools are sites for important social, personal, and cultural identity development (Lynn & Parker, 2006), it is critical that picture books used in schools form the foundation for language and literacy education that promotes the following:

1. children's social, cultural, and linguistic identity development
2. early reading and writing development
3. creativity and imagination
4. overall intellectual growth
5. a love for learning

## AUDIENCE

This book is intended for preschool, transitional kindergarten, and kindergarten educators at all levels of experience (novice to veteran) and background. It focuses on understanding and teaching picture books with social justice and equity content and messages, a foundational area of language and literacy education for all educators in classrooms, home settings, and community contexts. Given the cultural and linguistic diversity in our schools, and the frequent transnational communication of many children and families who keep in touch through voice, text, and visuals with relatives in other global contexts, this book's approach to children's literature and social justice is also designed to support multilingualism, cross-cultural practices, and family well-being.

We also conceptualized this book for preservice and inservice early childhood and primary grade teacher educators who teach courses on early literacy, language arts, and multilingualism across the preschool through kindergarten span. We hope it will serve teacher educators as a resource book for up-to-date theory, research, and practice on linking children's picture books with social justice and equity.

The book can also be used for professional development, professional learning communities, inquiry groups, and for book clubs. As researchers and teacher educators ourselves, we know it's valuable to have books and resources that span the traditional boundaries of preschool and the early primary grades. We also realize the challenges and the benefits of writing a book on early literacy that integrates theory and research from a variety of fields of study—sociolinguistics, children's literature, the creative arts, social justice and equity, antiracism and antibias education, developmentally appropriate practice, and culturally responsive education. In light of the book's integration of key ideas from these varied fields and approaches, we encourage readers to adapt and implement practical strategies that support your particular sociocultural and educational contexts.

## AUTHORS AND CONTRIBUTORS

Although Iliana, Isauro, and Daniel have collaborated and worked together for several years on various research, teaching, and professional projects and activities, this is our first coauthored book, and we view this book as a new chapter in our continuing journey in personal and professional dialogue, collaboration, and discovery. Each of us has also worked in varying capacities with our contributors, Laura Cardona Berrio, Maria Leija, Toni Sturdivant, and Patricia Sullivan, and it has been a pleasure and an honor to work with them on this book. Readers will note that many of the examples of linking social justice and children's picture books are from educational contexts in our primary home states of California and Texas, two states that contrast in terms of literacy curricula and policies.

## ORGANIZATION OF THE BOOK

The book is divided into three main parts: foundational ideas (Chapters 1–2), literacy through social justice and equity (Chapters 3–5), and curricular integration (Chapters 6–8).

Chapter 1, written by Daniel Meier, outlines foundational theory, research, and practice to highlight key forms and functions of children's literature with social justice and equity content and messages. The chapter provides a working definition of social justice and equity as connected with children's picture books and examines the longstanding role of picture books in children's language and literacy development. The chapter also discusses several key theory-to-practice dimensions for linking picture books with elements of social justice and equity; these include selecting books that resonate with children, using books that stimulate children's curiosity and imagination, supporting children's multilingual growth, and supporting children's early language and literacy knowledge and skills.

Chapter 2, written by Patricia Sullivan, examines key ideas and strategies for promoting meaningful discussions about picture books to promote equity and social justice. The chapter tells the story of how and why Patricia and her colleagues supported one child's interest in the concept of fairness through his passion for baseball and the life of Jackie Robinson. The chapter highlights examples of ways to support children's meaningful engagement with picture books with attention to social justice and equity and to frame discussions with children based upon their life experiences, interests, and passions. A critical emphasis in the chapter is the addressing of racism and bias through the lens of fairness, and the nurturing of collaborative discussions to support children's problem-solving skills for social change in schools and society.

Toni Sturdivant's Chapter 3 examines the use of picture books for planning authentic, play-based activities to promote racial identity. The chapter argues that culturally sustaining preschool classrooms are critical for forming attitudes toward diversity and difference. Teachers' beliefs, pedagogical practices, and discourse surrounding race in early childhood classrooms influence young children who are developing their racial identities. This chapter specifically focuses on how teachers can use picture books with social justice content to promote positive racial identity needs of Black children. To validate the experiences of Black children during their conversation and play, it is vital to select and use picture books with Black main characters living authentic Black lives.

Chapter 4, written by Iliana Alanís, focuses on making powerful connections between social justice, equity, and multilingualism. The chapter highlights foundational theory and research about children's multilingual learning and shows how picture books with social justice and equity content can support children's multilingualism and multiliteracies based upon varied language models and approaches. The chapter profiles the philosophies and approaches of teachers who successfully use picture books to make powerful connections between social justice, equity, and multilingualism. This chapter also includes a table outlining key criteria and strategies for selecting high-quality picture books with transformative social justice and equity content and storylines.

Laura Cardona Berrio and Maria Leija's Chapter 5 looks at emergent bilinguals' language and literacy in dual language classrooms through picture book read-alouds with social justice content and messages. The chapter identifies read-alouds as an equitable practice for promoting oral language development, which is highly predictive of successful, long-term reading comprehension. As children develop more lexical knowledge, they refine the concepts and ideas those words represent as well as their knowledge of the world.

Isauro M. Escamilla's Chapter 6 focuses on practical strategies for linking family engagement with picture books for social justice and equity. Examples from transitional and kindergarten classrooms show developmentally appropriate and culturally responsive ways that teachers can invite members of children's extended families to participate in picture books used in the classroom. The chapter also details strategies for allowing families to engage with picture books in their home languages and literacies, and to contribute their own ideas, feelings, dictation, writing, and photographs to the picture books. It is a valuable process for family members to engage with their young children around picture books and cocreate artistic products that highlight social justice and equity messages.

Iliana Alanís is the author of Chapter 7, which discusses how picture books can be used to amplify social justice and equity content in classrooms that feature emergent curriculum, project-based learning, and theme-based learning. Through examples from early childhood teachers, the chapter describes how active, child-centered curricular approaches can utilize picture books to center equity and social justice in the classroom. The chapter looks at using picture books as artifacts in dramatic play areas, integrating picture books with small group book sharing and discussion, children's dictation as linked with picture books, early writing in personal journals, drawing and art-based projects, author studies, and theme content as linked with specific picture books.

Chapter 8, written by Isauro M. Escamilla, examines the value of teacher inquiry, documentation, and reflection for linking picture books, social justice and equity, and authentic assessment measures. The chapter describes collecting assessment data through informal observations and written observations, journaling, audiotaping of children's conversations, and videotaping of children's interactions and nonverbal communication, and through children's play and work samples and teacher-created artifacts. In terms of the representation of this assessment data in classrooms, the chapter discusses the use of learning stories as conceptualized and implemented by educators in Aotearoa/New Zealand, ongoing multimodal documentation of children's engagement as articulated and designed by educators from Reggio Emilia, Italy, and the use of textual and visual stories as emphasized in the critical ethnographic action research approach from Oaxaca, Mexico.

## A CLOSING NOTE TO READERS

Just as when we read and engage with an engrossing picture book, we hope that our book immerses you in a new world of story, setting, plot, characters, and visuals that transport you to new levels of experience, understanding, and action. We have included beginning-of-chapter objectives and end-of-chapter "try this!" ideas in each chapter, and we encourage you to read and interact with this book as you see fit, looking for and reflecting on its ideas and practices that most deeply resonate with you and your work. We hope that you enjoy the book, that it deepens and broadens your practice, and that you keep it as a key acquisition for your professional library.

## CHAPTER 1

# Children's Picture Books, Social Justice, and Equity

*Daniel Meier*

We need to flood our own media with diversity. Many adults say, "Yes, yes, we need diversity!" but then they go back and read the same genre that they always read every single day and they don't bring it into their own lives. Kids will notice if you don't read diverse materials! That is so much more powerful than anything you can say to a kid.

There was a library that I visited years ago and saw a display of a librarian's favorite books. There were no people of color on the display—there were more cats than people of color!

As adults, we need to set an example and diversify our own reading so that we get to understand, "Oh! This a viewpoint that I had never thought of before," We truly see what "window" and "mirror" means when we diversify our own reading.

—Grace Lin (Amberg, 2022)

## Chapter Objectives

1. Describe key elements of high-quality and engaging children's picture books.
2. Discuss critical approaches and dimensions for selecting and using picture books that incorporate social justice and equity ideas, topics, and content.
3. Share examples of selected picture books that feature social justice and equity, and highlight key elements of authorship, visuals, language, voice, and content.

Picture books play central roles in effective and socially conscious language and literacy education for children in preschool, transitional kindergarten, and kindergarten. When teachers and schools consistently use high-quality, meaningful, and engaging picture books with social justice and equity content and visuals, this affirms children's identities not only as emergent readers and writers, but as emergent agents for social and community change. In this chapter, I describe and discuss several key theory-to-practice dimensions for linking picture books with elements of social justice and equity:

- Children are motivated to engage with picture books that resonate with their daily realities, hopes, and dreams.
- Children connect with picture books as well-told stories that stimulate children's creativity, curiosity, and imagination.
- Children engage with picture books that validate, respect, and uplift children's multilingual talents and interests.
- Children benefit from varied genres of children's picture books that move beyond the traditional fiction/nonfiction binary.
- Children benefit from multimodal ways of learning for accessing and making meaning from children's books with social justice and equity content.
- Children benefit from picture books that break down dominant narratives of certain languages and cultures as inferior and representing the Other.
- Children benefit from picture books that uplift their immediate communities and provide a vision for a sustainable environment and future.

Taken together, these key dimensions provide the foundation for educators to select and use powerful picture books to affirm children's emerging identities as individuals and as contributing members of classrooms, schools, families, and communities.

## CRITICAL THEORY AND CHILDREN'S PICTURE BOOKS

Critical theory and frameworks focused on social justice and equity address several key dimensions of children's social–emotional, cultural, spiritual, intellectual, linguistic, and physical development and learning. This book takes a holistic and strengths-based perspective on the value of linking social justice and equity ideas, theories, and research with the tangible and concrete use of children's picture books in classrooms and other educational and learning contexts (Souto-Manning & Turner, 2022). As pointed out in the book's introduction, as schools and society become more complex and interconnected, elements of social justice and equity must become more embedded in school, family, community, and online discourse through traditional hard-copy books and digital literacies.

The definitions of social justice and equity, and even people's reasons for wanting to engage with social justice and equity ideas and practices, are of course open to debate and dialogue. It is healthy, then, for educators and families to have ongoing dialogue and communication about the benefits of linking social justice, equity, and picture books—as well as about what might be problematic. For instance, are there books with social justice and equity content that educators love using with children, but that might make certain families uncomfortable? What kind of professional development opportunities can help us to understand and support these families, and what kind of dialogue and communication can families engage in with their own children, other families, and educators?

In light of the current deepening tensions and divisions in our society and educational system, it is more important than ever to address the full range of potential benefits of socially conscious children's literature and to consider the challenges in using these books with young children in classrooms. One key consideration is examining the current quality and quantity of picture books created by authors and artists of color, and of books for young children with social justice and equity content written by a wide range of authors and illustrators. On the one hand, over the last 20 years there has been an increase in writing, illustrating, and publishing books for young children about race, racism, power, and identity; on the other hand, we face increased book/author censoring and banning in schools, libraries, and in other public institutions. This book is intended to stimulate discussion and dialogue; we hope it may contribute to increased trust and collaboration around the selection and use of picture books for young children's growth and learning as agentic actors for democratic change in education and society.

There is growing scholarship on critical dimensions of social justice and on connections between children's social, racial, cultural, and gender development and identity. One key value of this work is the emphasis on addressing bias, discrimination, racism, and exclusion based upon children's and families' citizenship and immigration status and history, racial identification, cultural background, language use, neurodivergence, economic and housing status, and gender identity and sexual orientation. In bringing some or all of these elements into schools and classrooms, educators, children, and families can enter into an ongoing and evolving dialogue about historical oppression and discrimination, power imbalances, and privilege.

Influential scholarship on supporting the language and literacy learning of Latinx children, for example, has examined the conceptual and pedagogical value of LatCrit (Cantu, 2023; Solórzano & Bernal, 2001), which can be defined as "a theory that elucidates Latinas/Latinos' multidimensional identities and can address the intersectionality of racism, sexism, classism, and other forms of oppression" (Solórzano & Bernal, 2001, p. 312).

### Key Definition: LatCrit

LatCrit is "a theory that elucidates Latinas/Latinos' multidimensional identities and can address the intersectionality of racism, sexism, classism, and other forms of oppression" (Solórzano & Bernal, 2001, p. 312).

In this framework, Latinx children are viewed from a strengths-based perspective, celebrating and affirming their cultural, familial, linguistic, and social histories, talents, and identities. LatCrit views transformative educational philosophies and practices as based on historical and traditional Latinx family values such as resilience, spirituality, and transnational connections to families in other countries and regions. The framework also highlights the preservation and advancement of Spanish and Indigenous languages from Mexico, Central America, and Latin America, and the use of bilingual and translanguaging approaches in classrooms (Escamilla et al., 2023; García & Wei, 2014).

### Key Definition: Translanguaging

Translanguaging describes how multilingual speakers use all their language resources to make meaning and make sense of their multilingual world.

In terms of the implications of LatCrit perspectives for selecting and using children's picture books, "generative themes like *familismo*, cultural stories, linguistic pluralism, and elevating Spanish" play key roles in humanizing the curriculum, the instruction, and connections around picture books (Osorio, 2018, p. 6).

In addition to LatCrit, there are other critical conceptual frameworks that also feature selected elements and dimensions of social justice and equity that can inform our selection and use of picture books (Figure 1.1).

These and other frameworks are especially critical for creating curricula and teaching practices that support the transformative language and literacy learning of all children.

**Figure 1.1. Critical Conceptual Frameworks**

*Anti-ableism* (Harry & Ocasio-Stoutenberg, 2020; Johnson et al., 2024)—Anti-ableism is an approach that supports the selection and use of picture books that depict persons with disabilities with authenticity, respect, and recognition. The approach challenges persistent biases, stereotypes, and myths of individuals with disabilities.

*Antiracist and antibias* education (Bruno & Iruka, 2022; Derman-Sparks & Edwards, 2010; Iruka et al., 2022)—Antiracist and antibias education is designed to confront and raise awareness of the damaging effects of biases, stereotypes, discrimination, and exclusion of individuals and groups based on race, culture, language, gender identity, and gender expression.

*AsianCrit* (Iftikar & Museus, 2018; Yu et al., 2004)—AsianCrit has its roots in critical race theory, and emphasizes several key ideas honoring the life histories, values, beliefs, and cultural practices of Asian Americans to confront the long history of racial, cultural, linguistic, and immigrant prejudice and harm to Asian Americans.

*BlackCrit* (Wynter-Hoyte & Smith, 2020)—BlackCrit is also founded upon central tenets of critical race theory; it honors the linguistic, cultural, community, and historical traditions and worldviews throughout the African Diaspora and challenges historical injustices and harm against people of African descent at the societal, economic, and institutional levels.

*Black Lives Matter at School* (Helmberger, 2020; Jones & Hagopian, 2020)—Black Lives Matter is a nationwide movement protesting police violence and economic and judicial injustices against Black Americans arising after the death of Trayvon Martin. Black Lives Matter at School is founded upon central tenets of the Black Lives Matter movement, and emphasizes active resistance to racist policies, curriculum, and assessment practices that contribute to social and educational harm for Black children and families.

*Counter-storytelling* (Solórzano & Yosso, 2002)—Counter-storytelling is a dimension of critical race theory that challenges dominant narratives of oppressed and excluded individuals and groups in society, communities, and institutions. Counter-storytelling can take a range of forms: oral language, written language, music, other art forms, and digital literacies.

*Culturally sustaining and responsive pedagogies* (Paris, 2012; Souto-Manning & Rabadi-Raol, 2018)—Culturally sustaining and responsive pedagogies place the social, racial, linguistic, physical, and spiritual beliefs, talents, and interests of children and families at the center of the curriculum and our educational system. These pedagogies affirm children's talents and strengths and emphasize the power of social inclusion, cultural affirmation, and academic excellence.

*Disability studies in education* (Valente & Danforth, 2016)—Disability studies in education is an approach that emphasizes the full and authentic social, intellectual, and physical inclusion of children with disabilities in classrooms and schools. The approach also utilizes storytelling strategies to acknowledge and celebrate the talents and interests of children with disabilities and to advocate for their rightful inclusion and voice in the social and academic life of classroom communities.

As a foundation for any of these frameworks, we educators must move beyond seeing education as detached from class questions and as "raceless" (Jones, 2020):

> A substantial part of the socializing piece of early childhood education is to speak objectively to what all children need, such as, "All children need care and relationships." But nobody would say what it means to be understood culturally, and what impact race and racism have on the field of early childhood education. (p. 151)

The process of understanding the effects of historical oppression, discrimination, and exclusion is a critical reflective process for all educators across our careers:

> As Michael Dumas and Joseph Nelson pointed out in "(Re)imagining Black Boyhood," when we look at Black people's history, we see how their humanity has always been denied in a white supremacist society. And that doesn't start when they are an adult; it starts at birth. When we think of a three-year-old, we may picture a child playing, but for Black children, their bodies have been seen as commodities, and they've been denied that opportunity. During enslavement, Black children as young as three were made to work in the fields. (Jones, 2022, p. 153)

The personal and professional process and journey of broadening and deepening the centrality of race, racism, and power within the field of early language and literacy education must "center" the "magic, joy, resiliency, strength, and all the things that are wonderful about Black children" (Jones, 2022, p. 153). One of the key goals of this book is to link picture books with critical elements of social justice and equity so that this kind of philosophical, pedagogical, and action "centering" can take root and flourish in all educational contexts from preschool through kindergarten.

## CRITICAL ELEMENTS FOR LINKING CHILDREN'S PICTURE BOOKS, SOCIAL JUSTICE, AND EQUITY

Children's picture books have a time-honored history in the language and literacy education of young children in the United States and in many global contexts. Picture books connect us to our earliest history as human beings and the use of pictures, marks, and symbols to tell a story, to represent an event, and to communicate with others. Some of these markings and illustrated stories, in cave dwellings, for instance, are tens of thousands of years old, and ancient markings on animal skin have survived that record stories.

Over the last 40 to 50 years, increased attention at the societal and policy levels to the developmental needs of young children has promoted the modern era of the picture book as specifically written and illustrated for young children. In the 21st century, children's picture books are a burgeoning industry in the United States and in many other countries, and picture books are now ubiquitous in schools and classrooms, homes, community centers, places of worship, and libraries. Almost every public library has a separate space for children's books, and many libraries have librarians who specialize in ordering children's picture books and who lead picture book read-alouds, puppet dramatization, and art-related activities. In addition, the last 10 years or so have seen a rapid expansion of digital picture books for young children to be used in educational, home, and community settings in the United States and internationally.

The spread of digital stories has allowed educators access to picture book titles that their school and local libraries may not carry. Digital formats support children's listening to books in a multitude of languages and allow them to read picture books in varied languages and scripts; children with disabilities can utilize specific digital features to increase their access to and enjoyment of picture books. Taken together, all of these advances in the creation and distribution of children's picture books afford educators and families access to an unprecedented number and variety of high-quality and engaging multilingual and multicultural books.

In understanding and critiquing books with social justice and equity content and images, there are four fundamental practices to keep in mind for educators, librarians, and families:

1. Learning about the backgrounds and identities of children's picture book authors, illustrators, and photographers of color and others who have a deep understanding of children and families from varied cultural, racial, and linguistic backgrounds
2. Increasing our awareness of key connections between text and pictures in children's books
3. Recognizing the role of language and voice in children's picture books
4. Understanding and critiquing content and messages in children's picture books

## Authors, Illustrators, and Photographers

Literature is a place for imagination and intellect, for stretching the boundaries of our own narrow lives, for contextualizing the facts of our nonfictions within constellations of understanding that we would not be able to experience from the ground, for bringing our dreams and fictions into detail, clarity, and focus. Books allow us a bird's-eye view of our own lives, and especially how our lives relate to those lives around us. (Myers, 2013, p. 11).

In the 1960s, a seminal article (Larrick, 1965) highlighted the alarmingly high percentage of children's books that depicted only white children and adults. When African American children and adults were depicted in illustrations, the majority of these books depicted African Americans in settings outside the United States and primarily in the time period before World War II. The article specifically mentioned the historic *The Snowy Day* (Keats, 1962) and its depiction of an African American mother and child, though it noted the potentially stereotypical depiction of the boy's mother. Although *The Snowy Day* was written and illustrated by a white author, the book has endured in popularity with children, teachers, and families as an engaging story of one child's independence and adventure.

*The Snowy Day* and other books featuring children and adults of color have spurred discussions about the racial, cultural, and linguistic identities and histories of the authors, illustrators, and photographers themselves, and the content and visuals in their picture books (Myers, 2013; Sullivan, 2022). An overwhelming number of scholars, educators, and families have advocated for children's literature to reflect children's identities and social and cultural lives in schools, families, communities, and even global contexts.

> **Books allow us a bird's-eye view of our own lives, and especially how our lives relate to those lives around us. (Myers, 2013, p. 11)**

A number of scholars and children's book authors have questioned whether authors who are not African American can write credibly and authentically about the lives of African American children, families, and communities. Indeed, while children's books written by white authors for African American children have a history dating back to the late 1800s (Capshaw & Duane, 2017), some researchers define African American children's literature as "written by and about African Americans" (Brooks & McNair, 2009, p. 134), and argue that "books by and about African Americans emerged, in large part, as an oppositional and creative endeavor that challenged the selective tradition in children's literature" (p. 134). Others have extended the insider/outsider debate to the work of the illustrator, arguing that African American illustrators bring a valuable insider's perspective to picture books and children's book cover design (Bedford & Casbergue, 2011). In reflecting on the idea that "the percentage of books ought to reflect the percentage of children of color in this country," Myers (2013) notes that he "is less interested in that simple mirroring" (p. 11) than in honoring his responsibility "to make images, to tell stories, to trouble the narratives that pervade so many people's secret hearts and minds" (p. 13).

In terms of social justice content and visuals for children and adults with disabilities, Alexandra de Martini (personal communication, May 3, 2025), an early childhood educator who has low vision, points out that children's books about people with disabilities fall into three groups: (1) People with disabilities are portrayed as villains, (2) people with disabilities must prove their worth, and (3) all identities and abilities are acknowledged and celebrated. De Martini also believes that writers and authors with disabilities must play central roles in creating picture books with authentic and accurate content and pictures focusing on children and adults with disabilities. "Books written by and/or in collaboration with people with disabilities include fewer stereotypes and inaccuracies written by nondisabled people." De Martini also points to the value of authors and illustrators who do not have disabilities working with individuals who do, as in *All the Way to the Top: How One Girl's Fight for Americans with Disabilities Changed Everything* (Pimentel, 2020), as the author consulted with the main character, Jennifer Keelan-Chaffins, to make her story as accurate as possible.

## Visuals and Pictures

> Some of you might have already seen part of my story about my journey through books in *Dreamers*. I was someone who loved to draw since I was a little kid. Those drawings that you see in *Dreamers* are actually my drawings that I made, sometimes next to my mother's sewing machine; she would bring me paper and pencil so that I would not get bored while she was working. When I was growing up in Mexico, I didn't have books. What we had were magazines, comic books. I admired them so much. They were my literature. I admired the artwork, which wasn't necessarily for children, but showed me that if you were an artist, you could create things like what I saw on those pages.
>
> —Yuyi Morales (2022, p. 2)

As we consider how we can expand our knowledge of social justice and equity in picture books, there are a number of foundational questions we can ask regarding the basic forms and functions of visuals and pictures in children's picture books (Figure 1.2).

**Figure 1.2. Forms and Functions of Visuals**

- What is the effect on the young listener and reader of a picture book with illustrations versus photographs?
- What is the effect of digitally created illustrations versus those created by hand?
- What is the effect of photographs that have been digitally manipulated?
- What is the value of using the term *pictures* for the visuals in a picture book?
- What is the effect and value of separate pictures on each page versus one large picture on a double-page spread?
- How do visuals (whether handmade, digitally created, or photographic) in a picture book tell a story on their own?
- What is the visual and storytelling power of a wordless picture book?
- What are the effects of color and the author's artistic materials and media in rendering a book's pictures?
- How do picture books combine text and pictures to tell an integrated story?
- How do the visuals support children's cultural, linguistic, and personal talents and interests?
- What expectations or biases might be associated with the covers of books?
- What is the effect of book awards, such as a Caldecott Honor or a Coretta Scott King award?
- What can we learn about an author/illustrator or illustrator's style, medium, and artistic process from their websites and other online and print sources?

Let's look at one picture book to see how visuals and pictures convey and support elements of social justice and equity. Christian Robinson's (2019a) *another* is a wordless picture book that tells the story of a main character, a young girl of color, who is awakened from her bed by a toy mouse and her two cats. She follows the animals and goes on a journey through holes and up and down stairs, encounters other children playing outside, finds one of her cats, and eventually returns to her bed in her room. The story is told in Robinson's inimitable style of sparely drawn human figures, vibrant colors set against contrast backgrounds, geometrical shapes, spare plot, a mix of single- and double-page pictures, and a joyful rendering of children at play, moving, socializing, discovering, and seeking joy, comfort, and freedom.

As it is a wordless picture book, we can make up any storyline and text with Robinson's book, on our own and with children, and we can tinker with the potential social justice and equity content as conveyed through the visuals as we feel children will benefit. The main character is so independent! She is strong and adventurous! She seeks out and enjoys engaging with other children in public spaces! The story is democratic and civic-minded in a socially and communally conscious sense, and at the same time, it's a story of a self-empowered child following her own creativity, imagination, and sense of adventure. And it's a story of love of self and others, replete with scenes of "self-examination" (taking a journey in time, space, and manner), "interconnectedness" (out in the community with the child collective), and "liberation" (a world free of adult control) (Wynter-Hoyte et al., 2021, p. 275).

## Language and Voice

I always think of my audience, but never think for my audience.

—Mo Willems

Language and voice are foundational literary and linguistic elements of high-quality and engaging children's picture books, and they can play pivotal roles in emphasizing and extending social justice and equity ideas, feelings, images, and actions. There are several key questions that we can ask ourselves to raise our awareness and understanding of the power of voice and language in children's picture books with social justice content and pictures (Figure 1.3).

The style and the sensitivity of certain authors and illustrators attract children, and over time we expect that these authors and illustrators will continue to feature the voice and language that attracted children to their books in the first place.

Let's look at another picture book to see how the forms and functions of voice and style in picture books connect with social justice and equity content and pictures. *Agua, Agüita/Water, Little Water* (2017), written by Jorge Tetl Argueta and illustrated by Felipe Ugalde Alcántara, is part of a quartet of picture books focusing on water, fire, wind, and earth. The text of all four books is written in Spanish and English, and each book includes closing text in Nahuatl, an indigenous language from Central America. I have used each of the four books extensively with preschoolers, who are attracted to the first-person narration told from the perspective of the nonhuman central characters (water, fire, wind, earth), the vivid and colorful images full of action and movement, and the underlying content and message of the books to care for Mother Earth and sustain its beauty and wonder.

**Figure 1.3. Elements of Language and Voice**

- What is the author/illustrator's sense of aesthetics and style?
- Which genres do the author's works reflect?
- What languages are used? Are an author's books all in English? Are some in English and some in another language? Are any books in two or more languages?
- Are the books wordless? If so, what is the value of educators, children, and families supplying and varying their own oral and even written text for the wordless books?
- Are there favorite characters in an author's books that speak and use certain words and turns of phrase?
- Is there memorable dialogue?
- Are there a variety of story structures?
- Do the books' content and images connect with children's daily lives and interests?
- Does the book encourage children to use their multilingual abilities to engage in discussion about the book's content and images?

In *Agua, Agüita/Water, Little Water*, for instance, the story begins "A mi gusta que me llamen 'Agüita.' I like to be called 'Little Water,'" and the illustration shows a yellow-orange horizon with a body of blue/purple/green water and large raindrops falling and making several large concentric circles in the body of water. It is rare in children's picture books for an inanimate object, such as water, to narrate the story, but the children with whom I have shared the book are immediately drawn to the ancient power and attraction of the life-sustaining element of water. We dramatize the movement of water and the children draw and dictate scenes and objects from the book (Figure 1.4).

Toward the close of the story, the text reads: "Soy Pajaro de agua. De gotita en gotita regreso cantando a nuestra Madre Tierra. Soy Agüita. Soy vida. I am a Waterbird. Drop by drop I return singing to our mother Earth. I am little water. I am life." The illustration shows a large water bird in dark blue flapping its wings; it soars in the soft, light blue sky. The children and I enjoy flapping our arms and making long languid motions to imitate the movement of the water bird. The style and voice of the pictures, text, and languages all serve to promote children's connection to water and inscribe a re/storying of the mythical power of water to sustain all life, including

**Figure 1.4. "A Rainbow Waterfall" by Iris.**

human, plant and animal life. In a sense, this book and the other three books in the quartet are stories of human stewardship and care for the world, a subtle, yet powerful call for children and adults to raise our consciousness of the critical need to address climate change so we can preserve the water drops, the ocean, the waterbird, and by extension, ourselves.

## Content and Message

The materials that I used in this book [*Carmela Full of Wishes* (de la Peña, 2018)] were a mix of acrylic paint, but also cut out collage, cut up pieces of paper. I think the thing that really sold me about the story was Carmela is sad because her family's been separated because her father had been deported. Well, I don't first-hand know what it's like to have a parent deported, I do know what it's like to be separated from your family and your loved ones. My mother struggled with drug addiction, was in and out of prison for most of my childhood.

—Christian Robinson (2019b)

In a well-told and engaging picture book, the pictures and the language(s) and the voice work together to entice children into a story world or a world of information that connects children with social justice and equity images, characters, dilemmas, historical events, social and cultural movements, and influential individuals and groups. Young children enter these worlds of social justice and equity through looking at the pictures in a book, listening to a read-aloud by an adult or older child, or independently decoding and reading a picture book. There are several key questions that we can ask ourselves in terms of the social justice and equity content and message of a picture book (Figure 1.5).

Children's picture books with social justice content and meaning cover a range of genres—from stories to poetry to information books to biographies—and can include languages and scripts commonly used in the United States and in other countries and regions.

**Figure 1.5. Critical Questions Regarding Social Justice and Equity Content**

- Does the book help children to understand and challenge racism, biases, myths, misperceptions, and systems of exclusion and oppression?
- Is the book's topic or focus historically accurate?
- Are cultural traditions and values accurately and authentically described?
- Are the story and/or information accessible to young children through children's book browsing, adult read-alouds, and independent reading?
- Is there a celebration and honoring of cultural and spiritual beliefs and practices?
- Does the book address events and histories of discrimination, bias, and oppression without talking down to children?
- Does the book portray children and adults with disabilities with authenticity, free of stereotypes, and emphasize inclusion?
- Does the book offer a message of hope and possible paths forward for children's agentic actions for social change?
- If author notes are included, do these notes include citations and links to other resources for adults and children to corroborate and extend the book's content and information?

A number of picture books pay direct attention to social justice and equity issues and challenges. For example, there are books that address voting, such as *V is for Voting* (Farrell, 2020); the 1963 march on Washington, D.C., as in *We March* (Evans, 2012); raising one's voice and advocacy, as in *Speak Up* (Paul, 2020); raising one's awareness of children in need of a safe place to live, as in *Finding Home—Words from Kids Seeking Sanctuary* (Agna, 2024); and the historical displacement and denial of self-determination and freedom in *A Map for Falasteen* (Odeh, 2024). Within this large and varied grouping of books, some books are more narrative-driven and feature individual characters whom readers are introduced to from the story's outset.

For example, in *A Map for Falasteen*, the book opens with the dilemma in a classroom where a small group of children are looking at a map on the floor, and Falasteen asks her teacher why Palestine is not on the map. Miss Baker examines the map and tells Falasteen that there is no such place as Palestine. In text and pictures, the remainder of the book depicts Falasteen's quest to understand why Palestine is not on the map as she queries relatives and shares their memories of Palestinian homeland. At one point, her mother tells Falasteen that Palestinians do exist and will continue to exist even if they are not recognized on a map.

This book is primarily a narrative inviting readers and listeners into a story world of Falasteen, her class, and her family and their history, and the book includes an author's note on the last two pages. (These author notes, often written for adults, sometimes for children, are becoming increasingly popular.) The author in *A Map for Falasteen* provides biographical background on her own history as a Palestinian and notes her childhood memory of waiting in vain for her teachers to tell the story of Palestinians. The author also includes informational text providing historical and political background on the reasons behind the absence of an official Palestinian state and homeland, and includes headings such as "Where is Palestine?" "What does 'occupied' mean?" and "Where do Palestinians live now?"

*We March* (Evans, 2012) recounts highlights of the famous civil rights and freedom march on Washington, D.C., on August 28, 1963, and recounts this historical event as a story from the perspective of an unnamed African American family. The book opens with a double-page spread of four people walking on a sidewalk by houses, as the sun is just rising. The next pictures show two adults waking their two sleeping children. The family joins others at church for prayer, then they make signs to carry on the march, board buses for the ride to Washington, D.C., and then follow the leaders (Dr. Martin Luther King, Jr. and others), and sing in solidarity as they listen to Dr. King's speech.

The book's visuals are big and bold, with lots of black, brown, blue, and green for the people and background of the march. This fictionalized story of an actual historical event told in text and pictures personalizes the famous march and offers an accessible way for young children to understand and feel that they too are getting ready to march and to hear Dr. King's speech amidst the large, diverse crowd. The author's end-of-book notes provide additional historical background and information primarily for teachers and other adults, which they could read verbatim or summarize in accessible language for young children.

## PICTURE BOOKS, SOCIAL JUSTICE, AND EQUITY—PUTTING IT ALL TOGETHER

> Anthony and Anita have been enrolled in my family childcare center for a little more than two years. When I met the pair, Anita was three months old, and Anthony was a little more than one. Despite our program's focus on nature and the natural world, and all the time spent on the study of squirrels, bees, and crows in our nearby park, Anthony has consistently selected books with pictures of human faces. Anita is also a social reader, though the book is only part of her process. For both Anthony and Anita, reading is about a lot more than decoding: it's about coming to terms with self, identity, race, racism, gender, and sexism.
>
> —Patricia Sullivan, 2022, p. 54

If we are to center children's picture books in the preschool through kindergarten curriculum, we need a long developmental view of children's language and literacy learning, as well as of children's long-term understanding and application of social justice and equity ideas, principles, feelings, and dispositions. Achieving this is of course a pedagogical and policy challenge, and we need a new vision of what language and literacy looks like across the P–K span for individual children and for groups of children. In this new reconceptualization, children's picture books can play a key role in supporting children's holistic development and promote dialogue, collaboration, and civic and democratic engagement.

We can't let ourselves treat a curriculum that focuses on social justice and equity as only the icing on the cake; we must think of it as part of the cake itself. We must also, though, work diligently to link focusing on social justice and equity via picture books to addressing children's understanding, acquisition, and application of early literacy knowledge, standards, and skills. A thorough and sensitive curricular integration of children's picture books that feature social justice and equity illustrations, stories, content, and information is itself an act of social justice and equity.

Further, it is not enough to emphasize picture books with social justice and equity content if all children, and especially children from economically and racially marginalized communities, are not also envisioned as and supported as strong, capable, and invested storytellers, readers, writers, and thinkers. When thoughtfully conceptualized and carried out on a daily basis, there are a number of P–K pedagogical and instructional pathways that we can connect with picture books, social justice, and equity. These pathways are listed in an approximate developmental progression from preschool through kindergarten (Figure 1.6).

These early literacy pathways to support children's early literacy knowledge can be utilized in English-medium, informal bilingual, and dual language and immersion programs from preschool through kindergarten. They also can be used to complement optional and mandated assessment measures designed to help educators understand children's individual and group early literacy strengths and talents, as well as areas for further support.

**Figure 1.6. Pedagogical and Instructional Pathways**

- enjoying a book read by an adult or older child
- pointing to objects in a picture
- independent book browsing
- comprehension of pictures
- rhyming and phonemic awareness
- concepts of print
- letter and sound correspondence
- phonological segmentation
- early decoding/reading of isolated words and simple connected text
- beginning fluency and rate in oral reading
- early encoding/spelling of high-frequency words and short phrases and sentences
- vocabulary development in and out of text context
- storytelling, sequencing, and story recall
- text comprehension via listening
- text comprehension via reading
- early writing of varied genres of text
- sharing written texts with an audience

## CLOSING REFLECTIONS

This chapter described several key dimensions of creative, thoughtful, and engaging children's picture books with social justice and equity images, content, and messages. The chapter also highlighted several theoretical frameworks for approaching social justice and equity in education with potential application to children's picture books. The picture books described in detail in this chapter are just a few of the many books available for us to use with young children to promote a deeper understanding of inclusion, dialogue, community, beauty, creativity, and freedom. In the rest of this book, there are many more ideas and instructional practices for promoting this deep level of understanding and application, and we encourage you to find your own place within the remaining chapters as you contemplate the best approach for how and why you use picture books with children and their families.

## TRY THIS!

1. Conduct a book audit or survey of the books in your classroom or where you teach and note the quantity and quality of picture books with social justice and equity content, visuals, and connections. Older children and other adults can help in this search.
2. Select one or two of the critical theoretical approaches for promoting social justice and equity (LatCrit, AsianCrit, DisCrit, antiracist and antibias, and more) and find additional information and resources for how these approaches might support your reconceptualizing and rethinking of your use of picture books for social inclusion and academic excellence.
3. Research websites for authors and illustrators to find out their perspectives on how and why they create picture books and to learn more about their experiences and thoughts on how their picture books emphasize social justice and equity (see Appendixes A, C, and D).
4. Research online publications (e.g., *The Horn Book*, the Junior Library Guild, ALA Notable Booklist), online resources (e.g., the National Center for Children's Illustrated Literature, the Center for the Study of Children's Literature at Simmons College), newsletters (e.g., Nina Crews's, https://ninacrews.com/), book fairs (e.g., the African American Children's Book Fair put on by

the African American Children's Book Project, https://theafrica
namericanchildrensbookproject.org/), and consult your school's
librarian or a children's librarian at your local public library to
identify more books that feature social justice and equity images
and content.

## CHAPTER 2

# Engaging in Meaningful Child-Centered Discussions About Picture Books to Promote Equity and Social Justice

*Patricia Sullivan*

### Chapter Objectives

1. Discuss the power of picture books with social justice content and visuals to support children's out-of-school lives and interests.
2. Implement the cycle of inquiry process to support teachers' constructivist and emergent goals and strategies for discussing picture books about social justice with children.
3. Share examples of selected picture books that support and extend one child's passion for social justice, equity, and fairness.

## THE STORY BEGINS

Henry is a typical 4-year-old American boy. Henry (a pseudonym) likes peanut butter and jelly sandwiches, tic-tac-toe, and visits from our local librarian. He loves to run and jump and play with his friends, and last summer Henry fell in love with baseball and a story about Jackie Robinson. As his teacher, I had to ask myself: Should Henry continue down a path of myths and fables about America's pastime, or should this be the beginning of his understanding of social injustice?

Like a lot of 4-year-old children, Henry loves baseball. He got his first taste of the sport in the peewee leagues. He liked running the bases and sliding into home plate. And then his dad took him to his first San Francisco Giants game. There he was, sitting mid-level on the third base line with a hot dog and his own boat of garlic fries looking out at McCovey Cove, the red brick wall, and a sea of beautiful grass. His dad explained the game as they watched. Henry cheered when the Giants got a hit and held his breath when the opponents blasted a long fly ball to center. Henry got tired before the game ended and admitted he might have fallen asleep for some of it, but it was a great game, that much he knew.

When he came to school on Monday, Henry told everyone about the game. He was still so excited that his classmates got excited too. "When do they play again?" they shouted. "I want to go too!"

Mrs. Simpson, our local librarian, visited our class once a month as part of a citywide program to expand literacy for young readers. As a professional children's librarian, she is more than just an expert in children's literature. She is a performative storyteller with a wide variety of accents, voices, facial expressions, and a magic bag containing an endless supply of puppets and strange hats. When Mrs. Simpson came for her monthly visit a week after Henry's Giants adventure and asked what kind of books she should bring next time, Henry immediately shouted "BASEBALL!" and all the other children agreed.

As promised, Mrs. Simpson brought several books about baseball on her next visit. She brought a book that explained the game, with a lot of pictures showing how to play each position, how to throw and catch, and even how to hold the bat. She also brought a few picture books about baseball, and about children learning how to love the game, no matter who the winner is. And then Mrs. Simpson read a book about Jackie Robinson.

Henry had never really talked about the players by name before. He listened intently, asking questions and sitting close enough to get a good look at the illustrations. It was a long story with a lot of words so some of the other children lost interest and drifted away, but not Henry. As soon as Mrs. Simpson finished, he asked her to read it again.

"I must go to visit other children, but I'll leave the book here with your teachers. You can ask them to read it again, maybe later," she said with a smile as she stuffed her books, puppets, and weird hat back into her magical library bag. She was still saying goodbye to the children when Henry pushed the book into my hands.

"Can we read it again now?" he said eagerly. I could not refuse. We went outside and sat in the shady patch under the camellia tree, and I read the book again, just to Henry. I took my time, and he asked lots of questions that were difficult to ask in the bigger group. By the time we got to the end again Henry looked puzzled.

"Why didn't they want Black people to play baseball?" he asked.

"Back then there were a lot of things Black people couldn't do," I said, answering as simply as I could.

"But why?" he asked again. It was a simple question with a very complicated answer.

## BEGINNING THE INQUIRY PROCESS

Henry was due for his 6-month developmental assessment and parent–teacher conference to follow. Because of the sensitive nature of the topic, I decided to ask his parents' permission to proceed with Henry's question, "Why didn't they want Black people to play baseball?" Developmentally, Henry was meeting all the standard benchmarks and excelling in early literacy and physical development. In the parent–teacher conference, Henry's parents were concerned about his impulse control and his occasional outbursts of anger, which they believed to be willful defiance in response to not getting what he wanted. As teachers, we also observed Henry's occasional anger; however, we found that angry outbursts most often occurred when he felt something was unfair. Henry's parents confirmed that their inconsistency in applying one of their rules at home might be partially to blame for Henry's temper. We all agreed to include more conversation with Henry when he felt the rules were not being followed. Henry's sense of justice and fairness was triggered by house rule inconsistencies.

Henry's devotion to rules represents a common developmental benchmark as children begin to venture out into the world beyond their family, while holding firmly to the tether of socially normative expectations. His teachers have often observed Henry reminding his classmates to wait until they go outside to run or to wash their hands for lunch. As a master of house rules, he would demand explanation of any deviation. This is how I began to understand his question about Jackie Robinson and Black ballplayers in the major leagues. Henry needed an explanation for the restriction of non-white players.

With Henry's parents' permission to focus our talk on the exclusion of Black players in major league baseball, we began constructing our inquiry process, using the Cycle of Inquiry process (Broderick & Hong, 2011). As part of the inquiry process, I documented what took place at each phase of the cycle and shared this information with my staff and Henry's parents. The Cycle of Inquiry process is designed to be iterative; however, Henry and I agreed to move on to another focus at the end of the cycle (Figure 2.1).

### Observation

As a veteran constructivist educator, I know that children learn through their experiences and interactions with the physical and social environments they are exposed to. It is my job to help facilitate that learning by

**Figure 2.1. The Cycle of Inquiry Process**

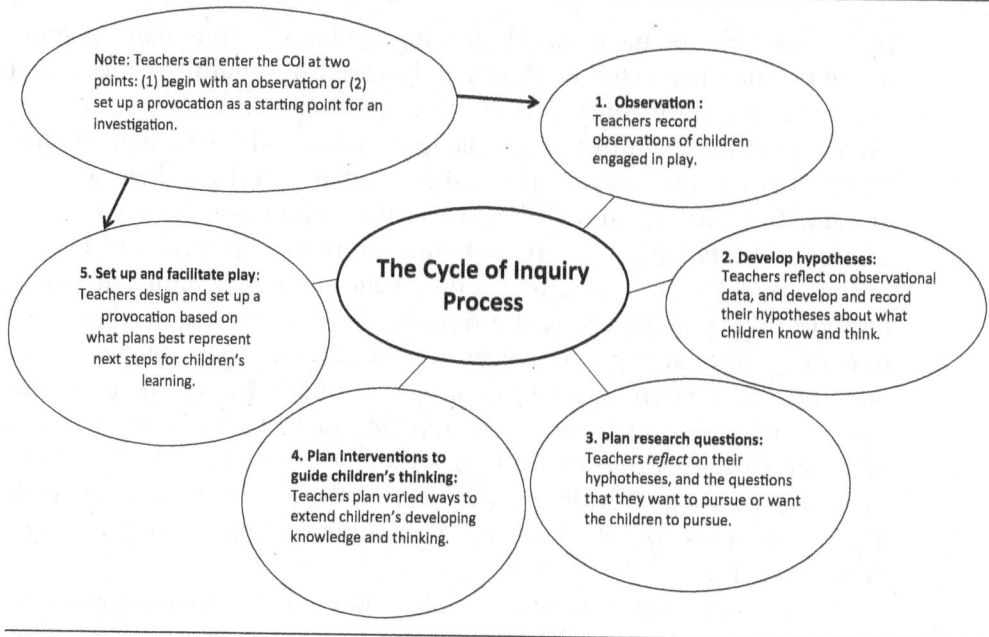

Note: Teachers can enter the COI at two points: (1) begin with an observation or (2) set up a provocation as a starting point for an investigation.

**The Cycle of Inquiry Process**

**1. Observation :** Teachers record observations of children engaged in play.

**2. Develop hypotheses:** Teachers reflect on observational data, and develop and record their hypotheses about what children know and think.

**3. Plan research questions:** Teachers *reflect* on their hyphotheses, and the questions that they want to pursue or want the children to pursue.

**4. Plan interventions to guide children's thinking:** Teachers plan varied ways to extend children's developing knowledge and thinking.

**5. Set up and facilitate play:** Teachers design and set up a provocation based on what plans best represent next steps for children's learning.

providing tools, guidance, and support. This was an easy task when we were talking about bees or crows, but now the question "Why were Black people not allowed to play major league baseball?" caused concern.

Henry is trying out his understanding of how he believes the world should be organized. He sees the world as a place where rules are created to make things fair. For Henry, the problem is simple. He is too young to understand the ethical dilemma created by a nation built on the idea of freedom and democracy while at the same time restricting the choices of a fraction of the population based on cultural heritage. But Henry understands that without the same choice to play professional baseball, Jackie Robinson didn't have the same amount of freedom that the white players had. Henry is developing a position on fairness well beyond his personal experience.

Henry is an only child, and his parents, immigrants from Canada, are only children as well. They grew up very independent. For Henry and his parents, their family rules were created through a democratic process, but with only three members on the rules committee, exceptions to the rules are frequent and confusing. When Henry began attending my Baby Steps Nature School, he became part of a larger community of 14 children.

At Baby Steps the house rules are all about safety, and Henry is a fast learner. He began to slow down when he was crossing the room, so he wouldn't step on the crawlers. When someone cried, he would watch the teachers quickly move to soothe and calm the younger children. He began to learn that the babies were crying because they needed something, and he decided that babies should be taken care of. It wouldn't be fair for the teachers to ignore the cries of the baby to finish reading a story or serving lunch because babies can't take care of themselves. For a while, a baby crying became an "all hands on deck" moment with Henry rushing to find pacifiers, bottles, and favorite stuffies in his attempt to help. Even in his most passionate games of chase, Henry will skillfully weave between younger children to keep from knocking them down. Henry's parents may have enrolled him in my school because we spend so much time outside, but what he has learned is fairness and consideration of others.

## Develop Hypotheses

I developed a working hypothesis that Henry is developing a value system that places fairness at the foundation. When we discussed what it means to be fair, Henry described three conditions:

1. Everyone gets the same amount (*equality*). If there are five cookies and three people want cookies everyone gets one cookie with two left over, unless we find a way to split those two cookies into three equal shares.
2. Everyone gets the same choices (*social justice*). We are all going to make Mother's Day cards. Everyone gets the same materials to choose from to make their cards.
3. Everyone gets the same treatment (*justice for all*). If I can't climb up the slide, then no one should be allowed to climb up the slide.

When comparing Henry's developmental assessment to the building of his three conditions, I found direct correlation between his responses, my observation notes, and three developmental domains:

1. **self-identity** (compares his own feelings to those of others)
2. **social/emotional understanding** (communicates how others are capable of choice)
3. **responsible conduct as a group member** (communicates group expectations and works with the group to carry out group expectations)

In all three of these domains, Henry scored above his chronological age. When Henry's development was compared to the assessment tool designed for kindergarten, Henry's scores placed him within the developmental building stage aligned with children at least a year older.

## Plan Research Questions

Usually, we begin our inquiry projects with a hypothesis, but in this case, I was unwilling to start with "What do you think?" For most children, and maybe some adults as well, it would be reasonable to ask, "What had Black people done to be excluded from the opportunity to play baseball in the major leagues?" I wasn't sure that I wanted to begin an inquiry with a question that would interfere with the inquiry before it even began, so I offered the children Henry's original question, "Why didn't they want Black people to play baseball?"

As a Black woman, I know a great deal about the history and treatment of my ancestors in this country. Henry knows none of that. Some would say it is developmentally inappropriate for him to learn about America's apartheid at 4 years old. I can understand that concern. However, framing the question from a perspective that takes Black people as the problem inaccurately suggests that Black people had the power to redirect a century of government sanctioned anti-Black legislation and public sentiment. By relying on Henry's original child-centered question, we could focus our inquiry on the rules of major league baseball until 1947.

Americans like to believe that our people are free to do and be anything they want if they work hard enough. We teach our children that America is the land of opportunity where rags to riches stories prove that hard work and good ideas will bring freedom of choice, and not just career choice but where we want to live, start a family, and send our children to school. One nation, under God, with liberty and justice for all. As the Declaration of Independence says:

> We hold these truths to be self-evident, that all Men are created equal, that they are endowed by their Creator with certain unalienable Rights, that among these are Life, Liberty and the pursuit of Happiness.

This is what we teach our children. This is what our families believe about their country and their government. What would happen if children learned that there were people in this country who were denied these unalienable rights? Would they ask why they were denied? Is it reasonable for these children to conclude that these people did something to deserve unfair treatment?

It has taken me a lifetime of personal experiences, history lectures, visits to art galleries and museums, hundreds of books, poems, and songs, and I still don't understand how a nation dedicated to freedom could so wholeheartedly embrace the inhumane treatment of Black people. I certainly did not have enough time to start Henry on a deep investigative process of learning about systemic inequities in American society. The question of why Black people had been stripped of their rights and humanity isn't the question he asked. The question was less about motives and maybe more about process.

Exploring Jim Crow laws can't be as complicated as explaining why they existed, but if this were an inquiry project for the benefit of Henry's development, how was I going to make it valuable to him? How does this project connect to Henry's question and his devotion to fairness?

So for all of these reasons, I decided to focus our inquiry on Henry's question: "Why didn't they want Black people to play baseball in the major leagues?"

## Plan Interventions to Guide the Thinking of Children

We know that children who live within the structure of established rules, either at home or school (or both), have practice in developing self-control. Magda Gerber, founder of the Resources for Infant Educarers (RIE), suggested that even very young children can benefit from understanding consistent and clearly defined expectations as a natural developmental process that provides children with a platform on which they can build their autonomy (Gerber & Johnson, 2008).

If you ask kindergarten teachers, they hope children learn social skills before they enter school. This makes perfect sense. Children with impulse control, respect for others, and a willingness to put the needs of the group above personal desires are easier to teach and keep safe in school. Imagine how difficult it would be if all the 5-year-olds in your class came to school unfettered by the understanding of socially normative behavior. Your classroom would be in dangerous chaos.

Those of us who work with very young children recognize *pre*-social behavior. Before children can understand and accommodate social rules, they invade the personal space of others, use violence to get their way, and when all else fails, they go all in on emotional manipulation by dipping into threats, tantrums, and screams. If we allow this behavior to become a habit into preadolescence, children are headed for the penitentiary, not college. Not only will these children learn less in school, but they will also have few friends and even fewer opportunities. Even though these behaviors may be developmentally appropriate for young children, ECE teachers know that a chaotic classroom environment makes learning nearly impossible.

There are a number of things that we hope children learn before they enter school:

- How to share
- That violence is unacceptable
- How to negotiate differences
- To be respectful of others and their property
- That the needs of the group must sometimes outweigh the needs of the individual
- To honor your promises
- That you have a duty to others and to yourselves—even when no one is watching
- That the dignity of human life (all life) should not be used as a means to an end
- That doing the right thing for no reward has value and purpose
- That one's right to dignity and respect is no more important than anyone else's
- That the rules we have for others are the same rules we have for ourselves

Teaching children to behave in social settings is the best way to help children move through school. Even children with extraordinary privilege need to learn socially normative behaviors. The thing that makes adherence possible is *universality*. The rules apply to everyone. Henry would say this is how we make our classrooms *fair*.

As we began reflecting on Henry's inquiry project and his focus on fairness, my teaching colleagues and I began by thinking about the word *fair*. What does it mean and how does it align with our developmental assessments?

## JUSTICE: AN OBLIGATION TO TREAT PEOPLE FAIRLY AND EQUITABLY

> Justice: The obligation to treat people fairly and equitably.
>
> —Cambridge Dictionary (2025)

Baby Steps Nature School has a massive collection of children's books. As a bibliomaniac with more than 30 years of field experience, I have collected thousands of books. They line the walls in several rooms, spill out of baskets on the floor, and travel with us when we go outside. We even have a community library box out at the curb. No child is ever more than six feet from a book at Baby Steps.

We hadn't noticed it, but the value of fairness is so deeply embedded as an American value that it is part of our national collective consciousness. We discussed the stories we read to our children. Nearly every book is a moral tale that either supports fairness or describes what happens when people operate outside the rules (e.g., Grimm Fairy Tales, Marvel Superheroes, Daniel Tiger's Neighborhood books).

As we read to Henry at story time and independently, we encouraged him to find fairness in these stories. Was it fair for Goldilocks to trespass into the bears' home or for Jack to steal from the Giant? These simple stories made Henry curious: Was fairness something that came naturally?

Henry was still thinking and talking about baseball most of his waking hours, but we were able to add additional books to his reading rotation, starting with *I Am Jackie Robinson* (Meltzer, 2015)

This book is part of a series called Ordinary People Change the World, and it's written and illustrated in the manga style with detailed text and illustrations, dialogue, and thought bubbles. The story isn't entirely accurate (Jack never liked being called Jackie) but it also doesn't shy away from some harsh realities either. Henry asked about the cascades of vitriol from fans and players and how difficult it must have been for Jackie to be the first Black player. It was critical that he didn't react or fight back, which made Henry angry.

I had to explain to Henry that there were no laws that said Black men couldn't play major league baseball. There were laws in Southern states that required Black and white people to live separate lives, but Black fans bought tickets and sat in the Black section of the stands in ballparks all over the country. There were also white fans who attended games played by Black players in the Negro Leagues. Sportswriters compared the players in national newspaper articles read by both white and Black baseball fans. The Black ballplayers were not as famous as the white players, but they weren't invisible either.

"Some people wrote about what was happening, but there wasn't anyone to call to stop the other teams or the fans from being mean to Jackie. What they were doing was awful, but it wasn't against the law." I didn't talk about the death threats. I felt that was a little too much.

"Why didn't anyone stop them?" Henry asked, tears threatening to spill down his cheeks.

"In the end he won them over because he was a great ballplayer," I said, hoping he would see that one person doing the right thing at the right time could change everything. We watched the end of the movie *42*

(Helgeland, 2013) and Henry learned about Jackie Robinson Day, when every player, manager, coach, and umpire in major league games that day wears the number 42 to honor breaking the color barrier in major league baseball and the heroic first season of Jackie Robinson.

"I want to be great like Jackie," Henry said with a big smile. For Henry this was a story about making baseball fair for everyone. It was about justice. Henry's distress at understanding that fairness and justice were not always given was troubling for the teachers. He needed to know that when we find injustice, like Jackie did, there are ways that we can inspire change.

We selected some books to help Henry understand that many different people from many different cultures and lived experiences have used their voice to demand change.

***Enough! 20 Protesters Who Changed America (Easton, 2018).*** The librarian recommended that we use this book that tells of people who did the right thing at the right time and made America think about justice. From Samual Adams to the Parkland students, the author, Emily Easton, and illustrator, Ziyue Chen, develop a connection from 1773 to 2018 with stories of people like Harriet Tubman, Rachel Carson, Cesar Chavez, and Jazz Jennings. We read the short biographies in the back of the book about Woody Guthrie (I played him one of Guthrie's songs) and Ruby Bridges, who had to face an angry mob at 5 years old.

Through this book, Henry was able to see that it wasn't just Black people that faced bad rules, and that some people were still pushing for justice. How does a nation develop bad rules? Sometimes it is because people are afraid.

***My Lost Freedom (Takei, 2024).*** This is a story about what happened to American Japanese families as told by a little boy who grew up to become a very famous actor and one of the first Asians to be cast in a weekly television series in a role that wasn't a servant. Takei describes that awful day in February 1942 when his family opened their front door to soldiers. With very little time to pack, his family was taken to a detention camp, the result of an order signed by President Roosevelt. These families were held as prisoners because America was at war with Japan, and many Americans worried that their loyalty to their homeland was greater than their loyalty to their new country. George was born in America, as were his brother and sister. They were not immigrants, but America saw them as foreigners. Henry listened to this story carefully. Young George describes camp life and how his family was feeling about being prisoners in their own country, but when the American government came to ask them to serve in the military, they were reluctant to fight. Henry was confused.

I chose this book because the story was told from the perspective of the young boy, but as I read, I could see that Henry couldn't see the dilemma in the story. For Henry, no one should fight in a war, so the prisoners did the right thing by saying no, even though many Americans thought they were being "disloyal" to the country they had been protesting was their new home. Henry was happy when the war was over and the families got to go back to their homes. I didn't have the heart to tell him that many of them had no homes to return to.

## SOCIAL–EMOTIONAL ASSESSMENTS ARE MISSING EMPATHY

> The seeding of citizenship in the classroom is aimed at creating a level of civility in the community and building the foundation for breaking intergenerational cycles of indifference and apathy. They may be students in the classroom, but they are the parents, policymakers and electorate of the future.
>
> —Mary Gordon (2009, p. 9)

The teachers and I went back through our assessment tools and were surprised to discover that there is no measure for empathy. Most of the observable measures are focused on socially normative behavior standards that could make classroom management easier in kindergarten. However, no measures focused on kindness, empathy, or justice. Are these missing because they are difficult to measure or controversial? Not according to the National Association for the Education of Young Children (NAEYC; 2019b). Understanding the emotions of others and the ability to show empathy are necessary social skills that help children communicate, negotiate, and navigate all of their human interactions.

At a Roots of Empathy Symposium in 2023, Mary Gordon told the story of Paddy, a 9-year-old with a troubled childhood history living in foster care whom she met in a low-performing school in Dublin. Gordon (Roots of Empathy, 2023) was tasked with helping the children in this classroom begin to think about empathy. She brought with her a baby and a doll. She asked the children, "What is the difference between the little doll and the little baby?" The doll happened to be brown, so the children said, "The doll is brown, and the baby is white." For the next few minutes, the children named several physical differences, the weight of the doll vs the weight of the baby, and the clothes they were wearing. Paddy said, "If you drop the baby, it will cry." The children talked about the feeling of pain and the different kinds of pain we can feel when Paddy interrupted, "The baby is a human being!" The children began to focus on the reality that what it means to be human is to feel. Because of his difficult history, Paddy has learned the importance of humanity and the value of developing empathy. In her work Gordon takes babies into classrooms with older children to help them discover their own humanity. As Gordon notes (Roots of Empathy, 2023), "We live in an emotionally illiterate world where we can send people to the moon and back but we can't reach the fathoms of our own hearts." Gordon says school readiness is a mindset, not just a skill set. We have to value more than just numeracy and literacy; school readiness should also encourage children who feel excited, confident, and curious. It was empathy, not anything we judged on an assessment, that sparked Henry's previous knowledge about rules and fairness.

## CLOSING REFLECTIONS

Today, Henry says that Jackie Robinson wasn't allowed to play because of the color of his skin. Henry understands that Jackie was not the color major league baseball thought was the right color. Henry also understands that some rules and laws are not good for everyone, and there are people who insist they should be changed. Sometimes those people are successful and sometimes they just have to wait for the world to catch up, which definitely isn't fair. Henry doesn't use the word *justice*. He uses the word *fair*, which will work for him when he goes off to school in the fall.

Henry's parents are happy with the development of his empathy and his understanding of the importance of having rules. He still struggles with his disappointment when he doesn't get what he wants immediately, but he has learned the word *negotiation*.

Henry has an ethical worldview based on the principles of justice where everyone is treated fairly. He calls people who behave unfairly bullies, and I am sure he will see a few of them when he leaves Baby Steps. We have begun to talk about what he could do if he sees bullies at school. Kohlberg (1971) suggests that Henry will follow the rules so that he will not get into trouble, but I am hoping he learns how to follow the rules that are fair, negotiates to change those that are unjust, and remembers to hold onto his sense of justice, even when there are a bunch of children who want him to do something different.

He should remember Jackie and the courage it took to stand up for what he believed in.

## TRY THIS!

1. Try out one of the books that Patricia read and discussed with Henry in this chapter. What kinds of discussions would you like to promote around these books?
2. In using the books discussed in this chapter, as well as other picture books with social justice and equity content and images, how might you implement the cycle of inquiry process that Patricia and her colleagues used?
3. Patricia focused on Jackie Robinson and racial equality and fairness in this chapter because of Henry's deep interest in Robinson's story and life. What other historical figures, events, and movements are your children interested in exploring, and to what extent are they motivated to explore the concept and reality of fairness?
4. In this chapter, Patricia notes the thousands of books in her program and that children are never more than six feet away from a book. In surveying your classroom or teaching context, how might you remap and reorganize your books so that children are in close physical proximity to books? And how might you intersperse picture books with social justice content and equity in all of your book areas?

## CHAPTER 3

# Picture Books as Tools to Affirm Black Children and Counter Anti-Black Messages

*Toni D. Sturdivant*

## Chapter Objectives

1. Discuss the use of high-quality picture books to affirm specific attributes of Blackness for young children.
2. Plan authentic, engaging, and play-based lessons that foster positive racial identity in Black preschool children, and design ways to differentiate the lessons for diverse learning needs.
3. Identify how to use high-quality picture books to foster culturally sustaining practices related to young Black children.
4. Discuss how to use high-quality picture books to empower children to recognize unfairness related to race and begin to act to make change.

This chapter focuses on how teachers can use picture books to plan authentic, engaging, and play-based lessons to affirm Black children's developing identities and empower them to advocate for themselves and their communities. Given the social, historical, and political context of racism (Iruka et al., 2023); the persistence of anti-Blackness; and research showing that young children are aware of society's notions of race (Sturdivant, 2021a, 2021b; Sturdivant & Alanís, 2021; Winkler, 2009), it is critical that early educators take an active approach to promoting positive racial identity. Escayg (2024) argues that it is the duty of an educator to "uphold the humanity and dignity of the children and families in their care, while also promoting children's scholastic success" (p. 8). Given the dehumanizing effects of anti-Blackness and its prevalence in our society, countering anti-Blackness and affirming Black children is a necessary component of effective teaching. Educators can enact teaching practices that respond to negative messages about children in ways that create powerful learning opportunities (Iruka et al., 2020).

In my role as a researcher, I have examined young children's racial awareness (Sturdivant, 2021b); preferences (Sturdivant & Alanís, 2021); and sociodramatic play with diverse dolls, gender, and racial discourse (Sturdivant, 2021a), among other topics related to young children and racialized and gendered learning. Using those findings as a guide, I will demonstrate how teachers can develop practical play-based solutions that counter the negative social messages children regularly receive as they celebrate the richness of children's racial and ethnic differences across the curriculum. I describe how early childhood educators can read story-books with Black main characters living authentic Black lives to discuss Black issues and culture. These readings not only validate the experiences of Black students, but counter anti-Blackness while addressing learning goals from preschool to kindergarten.

## THE NECESSITY OF BEING SPECIFIC

As a mother to two living Black children, Ayanna and Zuri, and a scholar-activist, I have found that we must be as specific in celebrating differences as society is in denouncing them. As a mother of two Black girls, I know firsthand that my children, as young as 3, could articulate that their hair texture and the color of their skin were less desirable to some than their white peers'. The specificity in their understanding could not be met with vague assertions about all people being good and fine. They needed to hear that their kinky hair and brown skin were good and fine to counter the messages that told them that those traits were not. Resources that vaguely celebrate human diversity serve a purpose, but to truly counter anti-Blackness, my children needed to hear affirmations *for* Blackness, specifically.

There is great joy in being a Black child and much to celebrate and affirm within Blackness and Black culture. This joy cannot be overstated and should not be overlooked. Even so, Black children can internalize negative views about their cultural groups. In earlier work (Sturdivant, 2020), I found that preschool children were specifically grappling with messages about the increased desirability associated with light skin tones and the attractiveness of long, straight hair while also experiencing media that highlighted Eurocentric cultural norms and practices. While there is a place for broad messages about acceptance and the beauty of human diversity, there must also be a concerted effort in homes and communities to counter specific anti-Black messages.

Young Black children are aware of our societal views around race and often make decisions based on race (Sturdivant, 2021b; Sturdivant & Alanís, 2021). Wright (2018) argues that intentionally selecting books that are not simply read, but are discussed and used for activities, is key to supporting the developing psyche of Black boys (and girls). In the following section, I describe several activities that can serve as a counternarrative to anti-Black discourse, along with activities that highlight advocacy as children learn how they can make important changes.

## FOCUSING ON HAIR AND SKIN

*I see the books and other media that I create as portals of fun, respite, joy, recognition, and exploration, where Black children and families (especially) can discover and revel in the wonderful and evolving qualities that make them who they are. In this time, where anti-Black messaging abounds, my hope is that Black children will see their humanity and diversity reflected and celebrated in the pages of the books that I write. I believe that strengthening one's connection to who they are shifts power dynamics and paradigms, in terms of how we as Black communities and individuals navigate within the external world and define our own terms of value and non-negotiables. I encourage all children to ask questions, to explore the world around them; to discover and actualize the power that they possess within to envision and shape their own stories and futures.*

—Natasha Anastasia Tarpley

Even within single races and ethnic groups there is variation in the shades of skin. Early educators can take advantage of children's natural inclination to compare and classify as a way to talk about skin tones (see Chapter 5 of this text). In *Our Skin* (Madison & Ralli, 2021), the authors explain that skin comes in many shades and that children can witness this diversity all around them. The book also explains melanin, the history of classifying humans based on skin tone differences, racism, and antiracist activism. The authors explain that variations in human skin tones can be witnessed by observing "our friends." Early educators could use this part of the text to introduce a combined science exploration (observation and classification) and math lesson on graphing the skin tones found in the classroom.

**Figure 3.1. Graphing Our Skin Tones**

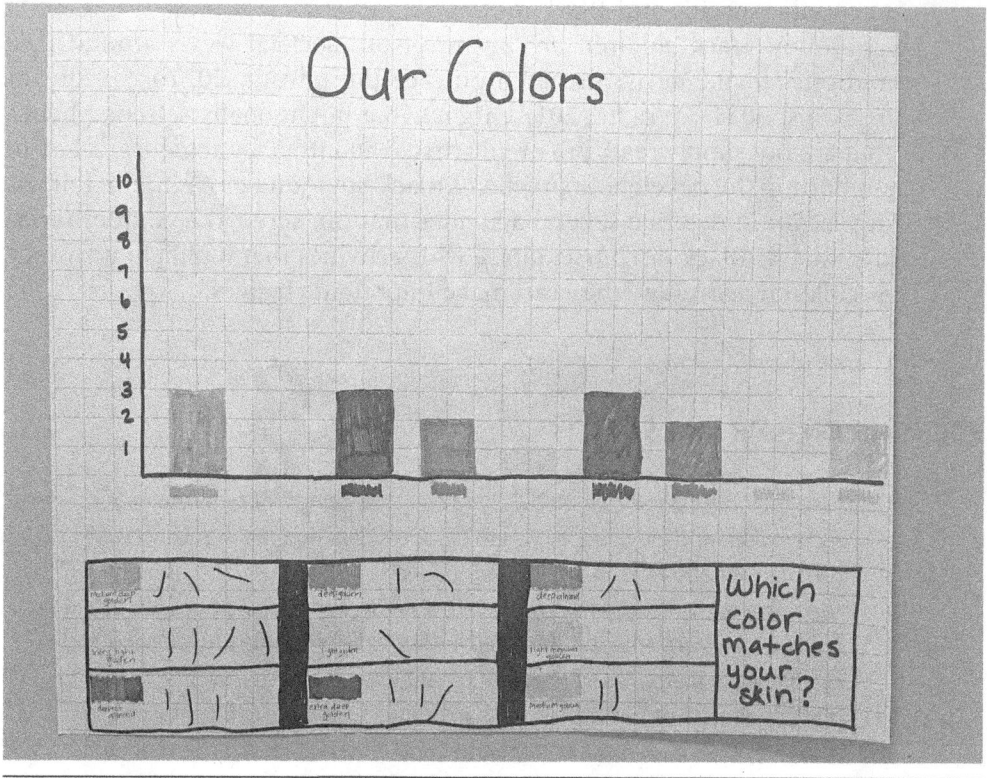

## Graphing Our Colors

As a group, the educator can make a graph with numerals on the y axis and shades colored on the x axis, using people-shaded coloring utensils, pictures, or pieces of skin tone paper (see Figure 3.1). The children can find the shade that best matches their skin tone, and the group can assist the teacher in counting the number of children representing each shade. The teacher can draw the bar for each shade on the graph after each shade is counted. At the end, the class can compare the diversity in the class by looking at the ways the colors are distributed.

*Mixing It Up.* Instead of creating a graph, each student could be given a clipboard and be instructed to put tally marks next to each color that their fellow classmate identifies as their color. Students can then pair up with a friend to share the results. Teachers can challenge students by having them write the numeral that matches the number of tally marks for each color.

## Syllabication With Hopping

In *I Love My Hair!* (Tarpley, 1998), Keyana, the child narrator, describes for the reader (or listener) getting her hair styled and moving through her community with hair like hers. Keyana describes using the sound of the beads to remember what she is to get from the store on her walk. She compares the sounds of the beads to the syllables in the grocery list. Early educators could lead preschoolers in a similar movement and syllabication activity by having children hop the number of syllables in items. Early educators could hold up play food such as plastic bananas, apples, pears, sausage, or other grocery-like items in the classroom and lead the children in hopping the number of syllables.

*Mixing It Up.* If children are unfamiliar with syllabication, the teacher could first lead the class in a discussion about the number of syllables in each item but emphasize each syllable in a slow pronunciation style. Once the number of syllables for each item is agreed upon, students could stand up and do the hopping game. Students could also offer words to hop that do not have physical representations in the classroom. This could allow more advanced students to suggest words with many syllables.

## Planting a Garden

*I Love My Hair!* (Tarpley, 1998) is a phenomenal example of a storybook that celebrates Blackness. Early educators could go to the book again and again and find many different activities to tie the book to early learning standards. One such activity could be planting a garden. In the text, Keyana compares the braids her mother installs to rows in a garden. Early educators could use this to introduce gardening or planting flowers in a pot. If there is outdoor space, children can assist with planting seeds or sprouts; if not, children can use quick-growing seed, such as beans, in small plastic pots to experience observing the living organism changing over time. Planting seeds tends to be a favorite activity for early educators and young children alike. Tying this common activity to affirming Black hair gives new meaning and expanded rationale to a classic learning experience.

*Mixing It Up.* If a field trip to a working farm, orchard, or plant nursery is an option, that experience would allow the children to witness the rows that Keyana described in the book. This concrete experience could make the figurative language easier to understand. Planting edible plants can lead to more engaging activities down the line and could tie in to the African American holiday Kwanzaa, which celebrates Black culture through the theme of harvest.

## CULTURE MATTERS

*When writing books, or designing curriculum, I put myself in my students' or readers' shoes—What would I want to know? Is this relevant to the culture? What would be engaging to me? But one thing that stands out is that my perspective will always include that of a little Black girl who grew up at times underrepresented and misrepresented. Unfortunately, a large majority of books and curriculum do not include authors of color—which often results in the exclusion of diverse voices and perspectives.*

—Dr. Kamshia Childs

African Americans have a rich culture worth acknowledgement and celebration, as it has profoundly impacted both American and global cultures (Morgan, 2016). Despite this, the culture of Black Americans is often mocked and demeaned. Even something as personal as the names families bestow on their children is a point of ridicule. Iruka et al. (2020) list the repeated mispronunciation of names that do not follow white cultural norms as common microaggressions toward Black children. Childs (2024) counters these microaggressions by affirming children with unique names in her book *I Am More Than My Name*. This picture book informs readers and listeners about the stress related to having a unique name in an anti-Black society, the gift of uniqueness that parents are striving for, and the unlimited potential of children regardless of their name.

*I Am More Than My Name* introduces young children to an important literacy skill while pushing back against anti-Black notions of cultural-specific names being related to intelligence. Preschool teachers could use this particular part of the book to celebrate names as well as to work on literacy skills through a small group activity around clapping the syllables in names.

### Clapping Our Names

Either in a small group or during circle time, have the children sit so that they can see each other's faces. The educator should then model saying a child's name, saying the child's name broken out into syllables, and then clapping one time for each syllable in the child's name. Following the demonstration, the children should clap the syllables in that name with the teacher. Once the teacher has demonstrated the syllable clapping activity and the child has had a chance to clap the syllables in their name, the teacher moves onto the next child and follows the same procedure. It is important that every child has a turn for their name to be featured. The game can be repeated until interest dies down.

*Mixing It Up.* The teacher could randomly draw names so the children would be unaware of whose name would be next. Students who are already skilled in syllabication  could serve as the model. The modeling portion could be removed once the students are accustomed to syllabication games.

## Heat, Wax, and Clay: What Will Happen?

In Sturdivant (2023), I discuss the importance of early educators and teacher educators tapping into ancestral knowledge as an act of anticolonization. When we think about affirming the culture of Black children, this includes precolonial African cultural knowledge and traditions. *African Proverbs for All Ages* (Cole & LaTeef, 2021) is a vibrantly illustrated book, with each page featuring one or two proverbs. The end of the book provides information about the origin of each proverb. Because of the complexity of figurative language, it would not be developmentally appropriate to sit and read this book from cover to cover with a group of young children. Instead, choose one proverb to read and discuss, followed by an engaging activity. The vibrant illustrations and positive portrayals of African people engaging in normal human activities serve as a counternarrative to dehumanizing narratives of Blackness and African people.

The proverbs can be metaphoric for example, talking about sun melting wax but hardening clay to describe how the same circumstance can have different impacts on people based on their own dispositions. Making the metaphor more concrete can help students understand how the composition or the characteristics of an object can impact how it reacts to its environment. For this proverb, early educators working in climates with high temperatures could have an outdoor experience where children have pieces of wax and clay on trays, tools for observation such as popsicle sticks, and hand lenses to examine what happens to these different materials in the same conditions. Following the outdoor exploration, the class could come inside and briefly discuss their observations and what the proverb could mean if it was talking about people instead of clay and wax.

*Mixing It Up.* The teacher could introduce other materials, such as ice and wet cloths, to expand the discussion beyond the materials mentioned in the proverb. The teacher could explain the proverb in a different way during discussion to make it easier to understand, such as how some people try harder when things are tough, whereas others get really disappointed. Educators could lead a discussion about whether trying harder is more similar to the hardened clay or the melting wax, why, and what way would each child rather react.

### Free Art: Watercolors and Patterned Fabric

Well-written, culturally authentic books allow children to see themselves, learn about others, and experience a new world (Bishop, 1990). *Going Down Home with Daddy* (Lyons, 2019a) is not only a book with an engaging and authentic story, but Daniel Minter's illustrations earned it the distinction of a Caldecott Honor. Early educators can use the story and the art to engage young children in an art experience using watercolors and patterned fabric.

**Engaging students in an interactive read-aloud helps to build lifelong literacy skills (Wright, 2019).**

Allowing children to engage in process rather than product-driven art using the readily available medium of watercolors, which was also used by the illustrator, will allow them to express themselves however they would like. Additionally, by adding patterned fabric and glue or tape, early educators can discuss the vibrant prints the characters are wearing in the book and how prints appear in cultural norms around clothing.

*Mixing It Up.* This open-ended art experience allows for learners of varying abilities to participate fully. If educators do not have access to watercolors, any paint would be just as engaging. If resources are available, children could also make their own patterned clothing with fabric paint or markers, or food coloring and plain fabric.

### EMPOWERING CHILDREN TO ASK FOR CHANGE

*Developmentally appropriate practice must consider the context within which the processes of teaching and caregiving are taking place. Today, early childhood educators are practicing within the context of both rising fascism and racist backlash against the movement for Black lives—in the United States, and across the globe. We wrote* Our Skin: A First Conversation About Race *because teachers and families said they needed tools to support the kinds of challenging, yet essential conversations that equip young children with the knowledge and skills they need to meaningfully participate in social change. Democracy requires much more than voting in a presidential election once every four years. Our hope is that this book, all of the books in the First Conversation series, inspire not only a lifelong love of reading, but also active citizens and healthier communities for generations to come.*

—Dr. Megan Pamela Ruth Madison

Children have ideas about how to improve the world around them and have opinions about what is fair and unfair as they naturally care about fairness in the world around them (Lee et al., 2022). They should be given the time and space to grapple with those thoughts (Kuh et al., 2024). Children should be given the tools to both articulate unfairness and be empowered to change it (Derman-Sparks & Edwards, 2020).

## Shared Writing: A Problem in Our Community

*We Care* (Madison & Ralli, 2024) was illustrated by Sharee Miller and provides a starting point for getting young learners to think about issues they would like to see resolved in their community. The text and illustrations give examples of common community issues that can be understood by young children. Following a reading of the text, early educators can work with a small group of students to brainstorm a community issue and then to write about it together to share with a relevant stakeholder. Perhaps students would like to write to animal control about a loose dog problem, or to the principal about additional recess. The activity is more focused on empowering children to ask for change than it is about dictating what children should want to see changed.

***Mixing It Up.*** The brainstorming for the shared writing could occur during large group time with different small groups working on their own writing about the issue. Each group could then share their ideas with the rest of the class rather than with external stakeholders. Children could also record videos about the issues in their communities and then draw pictures to accompany the videos.

## Dancing to "Lift Every Voice and Sing"

There are plentiful historical examples of resistance amongst African and African American people throughout history. Much of that work has an impact on today's daily life. One such example is the song "Lift Every

Voice," which is often referred to as the Black National Anthem. Lyons (2019b) wrote a children's book called *Sing a Song: How "Lift Every Voice and Sing" Inspired Generations*, which describes some of the historical activism that has taken place in the United States. This nonfiction story, written for young listeners, inspires children by providing information about the changes made by real people. The book features the song lyrics throughout and at the end of the book. Early educators can let their students experience the actual song in music form following the read-aloud. To make the listening session more engaging, children could be provided with scarves so that they can dance and move the scarves about as they listen.

*Mixing It Up.* There are many people within the African American community who know this song; musical parents or community members could be invited to come into the classroom to sing and dance along with the children. Children would also enjoy drumming along or creating their own shakers with water bottles and rice to accompany the song as it is being played.

## PLANNING TO AFFIRM

Picture books are excellent tools to engage groups of children, foster a love for reading, and teach concepts. The same is true for picture books about affirming Blackness and countering anti-Blackness. Early educators looking to impact the developing identities and thoughts on human differences have a wonderfully accessible tool in high-quality picture books. Here I provide some key considerations as you get started in your social justice journey to affirm the children in your community.

### Practicing Teachers

- Examine published children's books for text that can be a precursor or follow-up to future lessons.
- Actively listen for issues that children express frustration over during their play and then use them to have relevant conversations about fairness.
- Bring a list of your students' social identities to lesson planning to ensure an intentional focus on affirming specific identities along with other learning goals.
- Talk to families about how they support their children to have positive feelings about their hair, skin color, and culture and be willing to use their input or to provide suggestions if asked.

## Center Directors and Administrators

- Look for opportunities to involve children's voices in changes that will be made to empower children to speak up. For example, if new rugs are purchased, talking to children about their preferences before making the purchase will teach them the value of stating their opinion.
- Order high-quality books authored by members of the groups they are writing about so that educators can have a diverse, high-quality library from which to choose.
- Talk to families about how they would like to see their children represented in the program and what support they may need at home to make them feel affirmed there as well.

## Teacher Educators

- Work with community leaders to have university students present possible solutions to child-centered issues.
- Create class time and assignment objectives that allow students to practice incorporating ways to affirm culture as they learn to plan lessons.
- Develop assignments where students can incorporate affirming messages in lessons planned by their mentor or cooperating teacher(s).
- Have students think about assets for potential field trips in the communities that university students see themselves teaching and look for local opportunities for field trip grants so that student teachers graduate prepared to tie lessons into the real world.

## CLOSING REFLECTIONS

It is imperative that adults working with young Black children intentionally affirm their Blackness as they are developing in a society that denounces it. Early educators, including teacher educators and directors and other administrative staff, have a powerful obligation to ensure that their practices help all children see themselves as valuable, capable, and worthy. Vague messages about "all people" will not suffice. Adults can use tools like high-quality picture books, children's media, or even the community around them to send targeted messages that aim to undermine the lies about the inadequacy and unworthiness of Black children and other marginalized groups. In our home, affirming picture books, along with community cultural events, daily verbal affirmations, and honest conversations, helped to create a home environment in which my daughters learned to value their Blackness. This chapter serves as an example of how this work can be done in early childhood settings without creating an additional task on top of other teaching obligations by weaving together affirming messages and engaging, standards-focused lessons.

## TRY THIS!

1. Include real and authentic pictures and other representations of Black children with their naturally textured hair in the classroom environment.
2. Create a learning center activity where children use paint color samples from any hardware store to determine their skin tone. Children will enjoy comparing their skin tone to their peers' and learning that their skin tone is called Spinning Web, Spanish Moss, or Sable.
3. Have children use nonstandard units (e.g., paper clips, markers) to measure the length of their hair at the math center. As they do, they can discuss its texture, style, and color.

## CHAPTER 4

# Powerful Connections Between Social Justice, Equity, Multilingualism, and Multiliteracies

*Iliana Alanís*

Through responsive and equitable interactions, early childhood educators promote trusting relationships with children while building on their knowledge and skills. (Alanís & Iruka, 2021, p. 53)

## Chapter Objectives

1. Define and examine major theories of children's multilingualism and multiliteracies.
2. Identify critical pathways and instructional practices to promote children's multilingualism and multiliteracies.
3. Explore vs exploring ideas and practices for using children's picture books to promote children's multilingualism and multiliteracies.
4. Share vs sharing ideas for selecting and using picture books with social justice and equity content to support children's multilingualism and multiliteracies.

This chapter highlights key theories and research in children's multilingual learning to describe how picture books with social justice and equity content can support children's multilingualism and multiliteracies based on varied language models and approaches. I profile one early childhood teacher who successfully uses picture books to make powerful connections among social justice, equity, and multilingualism. I also share ideas for selecting and using picture books and include a table outlining the key criteria and questions for selecting high-quality picture books with transformative social justice and equity content and storylines.

### Key Definitions: Multilingualism and Multiliteracies

**Multilingualism** is defined as the ability of an individual to use and understand more than one language to communicate.

**Multiliteracies** is a broad approach to literacy that moves beyond traditional reading and writing, where learners encompass various modes of meaning-making. This includes gestures, visuals, audio, digital forms, and multilingual literacies (New London Group, 1996; Perry, 2012).

## LANGUAGE DEVELOPMENT IN YOUNG CHILDREN

Let's begin with a brief discussion of language development. Language is a vital tool for children to express themselves, converse with others, ask questions, and communicate their feelings (Otto, 2018). As a social tool, language facilitates communication and interaction, allowing children to express their thoughts and advocate for themselves. By exercising agency, children influence how others perceive them and how they perceive themselves (Wright, 2021). Through language, children construct their self-concept and develop self-awareness, contributing to a unique personal and linguistic identity. They establish connections and social relationships, shaping their roles within communities and fostering a sense of cultural belonging (Vygotsky, 1978).

Research underscores the importance of the first 5 years of a child's life for overall development, particularly in acquiring language skills (National Academies of Sciences, Engineering, and Medicine, 2019). NAEYC (2020) indicates that high-quality early learning experiences for children lead to long-term academic success. When early childhood educators understand the relationship between language, learning, and culture, they create equitable and responsive contexts and activities that are developmentally, culturally, and linguistically appropriate (Alanís & Iruka, 2021). While various theories exist on how children acquire language (see Otto, 2018, for comprehensive theories of language development), experts generally agree that language development is influenced by factors such as age, prior language experiences, and the home environment (De Houwer, 2009; Place & Hoff, 2016). I provide brief introductions to several language development theories in the following section.

## THEORIES IN CHILDREN'S MULTILINGUAL LEARNING

In this section, I explore three theories about learning more than one language at school. First, I examine Vygotsky's seminal *sociocultural learning* theory (1978), which focuses on the role of language in development and learning. Next, I delve into Moll et al.'s *funds of knowledge* theory (1992), which views families' assets as tools for developing curricula and instructional activities that connect with children's cultural and linguistic knowledge. I complete this section with the theory of *translanguaging*, which suggests that allowing students to use multiple languages in the classroom can enhance academic performance by enabling them to leverage their language skills to make meaning and communicate.

### Key Definition: Translanguaging

Translanguaging allows children to draw from multiple languages to understand and interact with content, supporting deeper comprehension and cultural identity affirmation (García & Kleifgen, 2018).

### Sociocultural Theory and Language Learning

While there are universal aspects of language development, educators must understand how sociocultural contexts influence the development of more than one language within U.S. schools. During the preschool through kindergarten years, young multilingual children are highly influenced in their multilingual learning by social, cultural, familial, and communal values and practices. These communicative experiences not only help children acquire language but also enable them to learn about themselves and others. Recognizing the impact of children's sociocultural contexts on language development is vital for ensuring culturally grounded and equitable practices for children and families.

Vygotsky's sociocultural theory posits that language learning occurs within a social context and through interaction with others (Vygotsky, 1978). Culture significantly influences language development, as children learn skills and concepts valued within their culture through interactions with others (see Rogoff, 2003, for an in-depth look at the influence of culture on development). In multilingual classrooms, children learn best when interacting with peers (see Figure 4.1) and with educators in supportive environments where their home languages are respected and integrated (Arreguín-Anderson & Alanís, 2019; Ramírez-Esparza et al., 2016). Language

**Figure 4.1. Diego interacting with Felipe.**

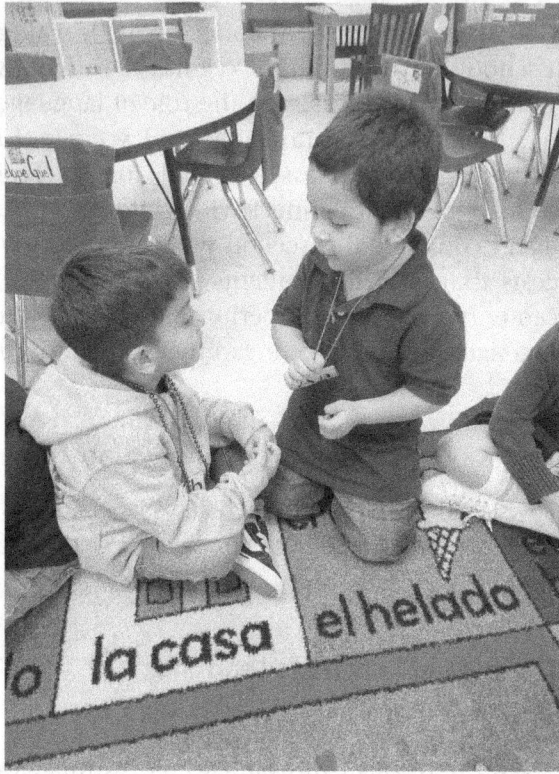

is a communication tool and a bridge connecting children to their cultural identities and communities (Vygotsky, 1978).

## Funds of Knowledge

The funds of knowledge framework emphasizes children's cultural knowledge and experiences from their families and communities (Moll et al., 1992). Moll and his colleagues argued that families of Mexican origin have various skills, knowledge, and competencies based on their working lives and community history. This strengths-based approach also fosters reciprocal family–educator relationships and meaningful family engagement. Funds of knowledge theory views multilingual children's unique linguistic and cultural funds of knowledge as assets that can enrich classroom discussions and enhance the learning environment as teachers leverage children's lived experiences.

When teachers understand a child's funds of knowledge, they are better equipped to create learning environments that reflect children's homes and communities. In other words, educators knowledgeable about the social and cultural influences on language learning engage in equitable and inclusive language practices (Allen et al., 2021) that support children's cultural and linguistic identities. They are in a better position to collaborate with families to create learning environments that leverage children's strengths and experiences (Alanís & Salinas-González, 2023).

### Translanguaging as a Multilingual Approach

Translanguaging theory recognizes that all people—monolinguals and bilinguals—have one linguistic repertoire, learned through dynamic social interactions, from which they select and deploy features to make meaning in context (García, 2009). Translanguaging describes how multilingual speakers use all their language resources to make meaning (García & Wei, 2014) and make sense of their bilingual world (García, 2009). Translanguaging challenges the monolingual notions underlying curriculum and practice through increased inclusion within learning environments (Osorio, 2020). The theory of translanguaging recognizes a language system that affords bilingual children more tools, richer resources, and flexibility to learn, express themselves, and communicate with others. As children navigate different linguistic and cultural contexts, proficiency in multiple languages enables them to negotiate their identities in various social settings, contributing to a dynamic and adaptable sense of self (De Houwer, 2021).

As a pedagogy, translanguaging is part of a socially just curriculum, allowing bilingual learners to enact different ways of knowing without linguistic constraints (García & Kleifgen, 2018). Teachers leverage the fluid languaging of learners to increase their engagement and strengthen comprehension of complex content and texts. Translanguaging pedagogies facilitate students' agency in shaping their bilingual identities (Arreguín-Anderson et al., 2018; Rowe, 2019; Seltzer, 2020). Recognizing the significance of languages in identity formation is essential for promoting a sense of belonging, fostering self-expression, and supporting children's holistic development (Sayer, 2013).

## RESEARCH ON MULTILINGUALISM AND MULTILITERACIES IN EARLY CHILDHOOD

Grounded in theories like sociocultural learning, funds of knowledge, and translanguaging, using culturally sustaining picture books allows children to see their languages and identities valued and reflected in authentic learning experiences. Picture books with social justice and equity themes offer unique opportunities to address multilingual learners' social–emotional, linguistic, and cultural needs. These books can enhance children's understanding of the world, build empathy, and, crucially, support the development of multilingualism and multiliteracies (Alvarez, 2018; Leija & Fránquiz, 2021). Children's literature offers structures and starting points for children to think about their racial and linguistic identity (Tager, 2022) and provides a foundation to further explore social justice issues as children build knowledge and continue critical reflections on racial identity with literature they can relate to.

## Multiliteracies Theory and Picture Books

The theory of multiliteracies, developed by the New London Group (1996), broadens traditional notions of literacy to include multiple forms of communication, including visual, digital, and multilingual literacies. Multiliteracies create a pedagogy in which "language and other modes of meaning are dynamic representational resources, constantly being remade by their users as they work to achieve their various cultural purposes" (NLG, p. 64). For multilingual learners, picture books provide a multimodal learning experience that aligns with multiliteracies theory by combining visual and textual elements that aid comprehension. Studies indicate that children link images and text to understand meaning, particularly when facing unfamiliar words or complex themes (Kim & Heyneman, 2015; Rowe & Miller, 2016). Using a multiliteracies framework to leverage students' linguistic and cultural backgrounds underscores the importance of adopting a multilingual and multimodal approach to support literacy learning. For example, multilingual picture books challenge common perceptions related to languages, such as the notion that all people speak English. By integrating social justice themes, picture books support multiliteracies by exposing children to diverse cultural perspectives, enabling them to understand the world through both linguistic and visual contexts.

## Social Justice Picture Books and Language Development

Research indicates that picture books with social justice themes can enhance young children's critical thinking and language development (Botelho & Rudman, 2009). Picture books addressing topics like fairness, equality, and respect for diversity enable children to engage in meaningful discussions that support language use (Wild, 2023a). In multilingual settings, these discussions encourage children to use both their home and target languages, reinforcing their linguistic competence and confidence. Souto-Manning and Vasquez (2011) found that preschoolers exposed to social justice themes in picture books developed empathy and language skills as they engaged in reflective dialogues on the presented themes. Teachers create meaningful contexts for language interaction with peers when incorporating picture books with social justice themes. This allows children to connect with content that mirrors their lives and promotes shared values of fairness and empathy.

## Picture Book Use in Bilingual and Dual-Language Models

Bilingual and dual-language models emphasize the integration of home and target languages for children's long-term academic success. Picture books with bilingual text or culturally relevant stories can help children draw parallels between languages, enhancing their vocabulary and understanding of concepts in both languages (López-Robertson, 2021). Research on dual-language immersion programs indicates that children who engage with bilingual books (see Figure 4.2) perform better academically

**Figure 4.2. Reading and discussing picture books.**

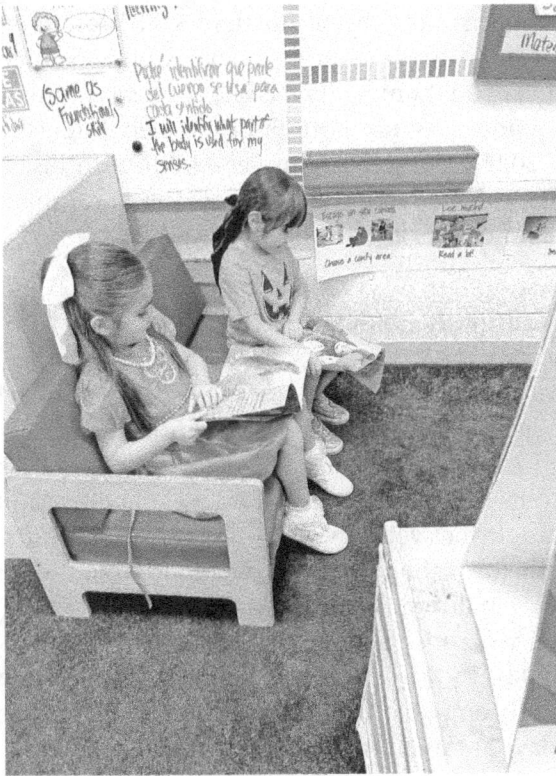

in both languages and demonstrate higher cultural awareness (Genesee et al., 2004). Naqvi et al. (2013) found that "providing young linguistic minority children with multilingual literacy exposure in the form of dual language books enables them to use their linguistic and cultural capital within the mainstream classes" (p. 522). Picture books exploring equity and justice themes provide an ideal medium for children to connect their home cultures to classroom content. This reinforces the message that their experiences and languages are valuable aspects of their learning (Alvarez, 2018; Leija & Fránquiz, 2021).

## USING PICTURE BOOKS FOR MULTILINGUAL AND MULTILITERACY DEVELOPMENT

When selecting picture books, emphasize those that showcase diverse cultures, languages, and experiences. Picture books highlighting fairness, empathy, and cultural pride resonate with multilingual children, making the content accessible and personally relevant. Some examples include *Tan to Tamarind: Poems About the Color Brown* (Iyengar, 2009), which addresses a spectrum of beautiful shades of brown, and *Mango, Abuela, and Me* (Medina, 2015), a story about family connections across language barriers. The themes allow children to strengthen their sense of self and identity and may promote pride in their linguistic abilities (López-Robertson, 2021). These books invite children to discuss complex social issues through developmentally appropriate texts that serve as catalysts for meaningful conversations.

### Incorporating Culturally Relevant Texts

Culturally relevant texts help students understand who they are and where they come from because they connect to students' lived experiences, not just to their cultural heritage. Preschool and kindergarten children are in the midst of identity development. Multilingual children are often caught between two cultural worlds. Culturally relevant texts help children form their bilingual or multilingual identity and promote pride in their bicultural world.

One of my favorite texts is Alma Flor Ada's *I Love Saturdays y domingos* (Ada, 2002). In this text, Alma Flor Ada describes the joy of a young girl's weekends enjoying time with her maternal and paternal grandparents. Saturdays are spent with her Euro-American Grandma and Grandpa, and *los domingos* [Sundays] are spent with her Mexican American *abuelito* [grandfather] and *abuelita* [grandmother]. This picture book reflects the family experiences of many multilingual children (including my son) who are developing their own identities as they straddle two cultural worlds. Children's literature that shares the experiences, contributions, and perspectives of various cultural groups can help young children develop a sense of belonging as they explore their cultural identities and experiences. My work with young children reveals that when children see characters who look like them, share similar backgrounds, or experience similar challenges, they feel validated and acknowledged. This serves to boost their self-esteem and sense of belonging in the classroom. Culturally relevant picture books offer an opportunity to increase empathy and push back against the bias and prejudice children may experience within their own schools and communities.

### Encouraging Translanguaging During Story Time

Educators can create an inclusive reading environment by encouraging children to use their home and target languages during story time. As a pedagogical practice, translanguaging affirms children's home languages and supports language and literacy development (Gort & Sembiante, 2015). When teachers use picture books with social justice themes, translanguaging allows children to express ideas using all of their linguistic resources (Kelly, 2022). This facilitates more meaningful engagement with the material and allows children to contribute to discussions on social issues through a rich linguistic lens. This approach validates children's linguistic identities and deepens their understanding of the story's themes, as they can discuss complex ideas using all their linguistic resources (García, 2020; Osorio, 2020).

By selecting picture books that reflect children's cultures and address social justice issues, early childhood educators can encourage cross-linguistic transfer and deeper engagement with the themes of equity and inclusion. For example, teachers might ask questions that invite responses in any language or allow children to explain concepts to each other using their language of learning (Arreguín & Alanís, 2023). After reading sections of the text, teachers can ask students to summarize with a partner using their full linguistic repertoire. This allows students to maximize their meaning-making potential through the connections they make across the different languages they speak (Leander & Boldt, 2013). It also creates opportunities for students to develop their multilingualism in multiple spaces.

**Key Definition: Language of Learning (LOL)**

Language of Learning (LOL) is the language the students use when engaging in discussions, group projects, or responding to the teacher's questions (Arreguín & Alanís, 2023). This can be students' home language, English, or both.

## SELECTING HIGH-QUALITY CHILDREN'S BOOKS

Children have the right to see themselves reflected respectfully and accurately in classrooms, books, and curricula (López-Robertson, 2021). As an early childhood educator, you must exercise care when choosing high-quality picture books that are culturally authentic, accurate, and reflective of the children in your classroom (see Appendix A for resources). Table 4.1 outlines key criteria and questions to ask when selecting high-quality picture books with transformative social justice and equity content and storylines.

## FACILITATING DISCUSSIONS ON SOCIAL JUSTICE THEMES

Picture books with social justice content provide opportunities for critical discussions about fairness, respect, and empathy (Harper & Trostle-Brand, 2010; Wild, 2023a). Teachers can ask open-ended questions that prompt children to think about how the story connects to their own experiences or to issues they observe in the world around them (Hawkins, 2014). This encourages children to articulate their thoughts in multiple languages, building their vocabulary and critical thinking skills while promoting justice and respect for diversity (López-Robertson, 2021).

Effective teachers draw on children's diverse linguistic backgrounds to enrich discussions, using picture books to validate and celebrate their cultural identities. Here I introduce you to Ms. Diana, an early childhood educator who incorporates books written by authors who represent various cultural, linguistic, and racial backgrounds and whose stories reflect the languages and cultures of the children in her classroom. She successfully uses picture books to make powerful connections between social justice, equity, and multilingualism.

Ms. Diana, a kindergarten Spanish-English dual-language teacher in South Central Texas, combines the art of telling stories with multimedia through family photos and digital storytelling. Digital stories use technical tools to blend audio, video, and graphics with the author's story and have

**Table 4.1. Questions to Consider When Selecting High-Quality Picture Books**

| Criteria | Questions to Consider | | |
|---|---|---|---|
| Examine the illustrations | What images are used to depict the characters in the story? Are they accurate and respectful? | Do people of color look stereotypically alike, or are they depicted as genuine individuals with distinctive features? | Are the illustrations integral to the experiences and interactions? Do they work together with the text to create meaning? |
| Read the storyline | Whose perspectives and experiences are portrayed? Check for age appropriateness. | Does the storyline encourage passive acceptance or active resistance? Does the book include struggles for justice? | Do people of color and women experience forms of oppression that are connected to social injustice? |
| Consider the audience | Who is the book written for? Are the characters about the same age as the children in your classroom? | Will children in your classroom see themselves represented in the illustrations and story? Can children put themselves in the role of the character(s)? | Can children share their stories based on the story of the text? Will the stories encourage discussion and build community? |
| Analyze the characters | Are the characters based on extraordinary people, such as heroes? Children should see themselves represented in the characters. Do they reflect children's cultural identities? | Are the characters from the here and now? Are they believable? Do they feature characters with diverse physical abilities? | Are the main characters depicted as animals? |
| Analyze the language of the text | Does language affirm children's self-concept? | Does the language have insulting overtones? Is the language sexist or gendered? | Will the language promote understanding of our diverse society? |
| Analyze the bilingual language | Is the language consistent, and is the written and conversational text correct? | Does the language reflect a natural flow in conversation? | Do the characters know English? |

**Table 4.1.** *(continued)*

| Criteria | Questions to Consider | | |
|---|---|---|---|
| Look for tokenism | Is there only one example of any minoritized group represented among the characters? | Will all of the children in your classroom see themselves and their family's way of life reflected in the book? | Avoid the invisibility of certain groups, such as homeless families and transgender children |
| Examine the lifestyles | Do the illustrations and text transcend oversimplifications and offer genuine insight into the characters' lifestyles? | Look for inaccuracy and inappropriateness in depicting cultures outside the dominant white society. Are lifestyles realistic? | Does the book depict diversity among people within a specific racial/ethnic group, such as family structures, living environments, socioeconomic conditions and types of work, and male/female roles within the family? |
| Weighs the relationships | Who has power or significance in the book? | Do people of color and females primarily function in supporting roles? | Are characters from a range of genders portrayed in nurturing roles? |
| Consider the author or illustrator's background | What qualifies the author or illustrator to deal with the subject? | Does the author's perspective substantially weaken or strengthen the book's value? | Who is telling the story? |
| Consider the quality of the book overall | Are the illustrations colorful and recognizable to young children? | Are there relevant storylines where different kinds of people are integral to the story? | Will children find the text appealing? Where does the story take place? Is it realistic? |

been a transformative technological tool in bilingual classrooms (Kosara & Mackinlay, 2013; Robin, 2008). Ms. Diana uses digital storytelling to facilitate multiple literacy skills through multimodal practices as children build on narrative skills acquired through practices at home. The interaction between traditional texts and new digital literacies creates a two-way process of knowledge sharing through multimodal texts (Naidoo & Crandall, 2011) and provides an outlet for children to demonstrate their creativity and learning (see O'Byrne et al., 2018, for more information on digital storytelling).

Ms. Diana intentionally selects bilingual books that reflect the diverse immigration trajectories of her students. She uses these books as a foundation for storytelling and identity exploration. As a class, they read *My Name Is Jorge on Both Sides of the River* (Medina, 1999); *Where Are You From?/¿De dónde eres?* (Méndez, 2019); and *The Boy from Mexico* (Dennis, 2022). These books recount the experiences of young children facing relocation, from one country to another or from one place to another, addressing obstacles and coping with the loss of a relative or a friend. Through interactive readings and discussion, Ms. Diana encourages the children to make connections between the characters' journeys and their own. She uses literature to help children see how they, too, can tell their stories.

Once the class had read and discussed the various books, Ms. Diana used Photostory, a child-friendly storytelling application, to help children create authentic multimodal narratives (Kress, 2010). The stories were created in multiple steps (see Table 4.2), and the software allowed students to mix video and still images, title, music, and narration. Children would first share their pictures, videos, and audio with partners (see Figure 4.3). Then they would draw or write their stories using traditional paper and pencils (see Figure 4.4).

Then Ms. Diana and her instructional aide helped the children transfer the story onto the digital platform. Children proudly presented their digital stories to their classmates, who provided comments and questions as they made connections to their peers' experiences.

Through digital storytelling, the children in Ms. Diana's class developed their digital literacy skills within a culturally affirming multimedia and multimodal framework. These creative digital stories enhance children's understanding of cultural similarities and differences, cultivating cross-cultural understanding and helping them successfully navigate their world (Clarke, 2020). Additionally, digital literacy empowers children to develop and express understanding in multiple ways (orally, digitally, drawing, and writing) that may have been excluded from traditional paper-and-pencil formats (Clarke, 2020).

## CLOSING REFLECTIONS

This chapter highlighted key theories and research in children's multilingual learning to describe how picture books with social justice and equity content support children's multilingualism and multiliteracies. Effective early childhood teachers use picture books to make powerful connections between social justice, equity, and multilingualism. They engage children in critical discussions about fairness, respect, and empathy using all their linguistic resources. Picture books that showcase diverse cultures, languages, and experiences resonate with multilingual children, making the

**Table 4.2. Steps for Digital Storytelling**

| | | | |
|---|---|---|---|
| The teacher facilitates brainstorming and helps the children choose a simple story idea. | The teacher focuses on familiar themes and positive experiences that are relevant for young children (reuniting with family members, birthday parties, visiting extended family, taking care of pets). | Children discuss their ideas with their partner. This allows them to organize their thoughts and formulate questions. | Following the brainstorming session, the teacher writes down the selected ideas. For example, Lucila visiting family in Mexico Marco picking oranges with his abuelo (grandpa) Mariela helping her grandma collect the chickens' eggs |
| The teacher asks families to support their children in gathering story materials, including photographs, videos, and audio. Families may need time to capture and prepare these elements. | Teachers invite families to email or text pictures, videos, and/or audio clips. This makes it easier to organize digital files for each child. | With their partner, children discuss the various pictures, videos, and/or audio clips they have selected. | Pictures that represent what children want to say can be found online if families do not have access to them. |
| Teacher models how to write or draw a story using a story-board. | Children use drawings and pictures to orally plan the sequence of the story with a storyboard. This helps them organize story events and understand narrative structure. | Using paper/pencil, children draw or write their story on a storyboard. | Children share their drawings and/or written stories with peers to help ensure they have captured every-thing they want to say. |
| Teacher and other adults help children edit and assemble the final product. | Teacher uses a child-friendly app with easy-to-use features to combine the images, audio, and narration. You can also use platforms such as Canva, PowerPoint, or iMovie. | Children review their digital stories and share them with their partner, thereby enhancing their confidence in storytelling. | Once children are ready, they present their digital stories to their peers. |

*Source:* Adapted from Derman-Sparks & Ramsey (2011), López-Robertson (2021), and Worlds of Words (2020).

**Figure 4.3. Sharing family pictures with a partner.**

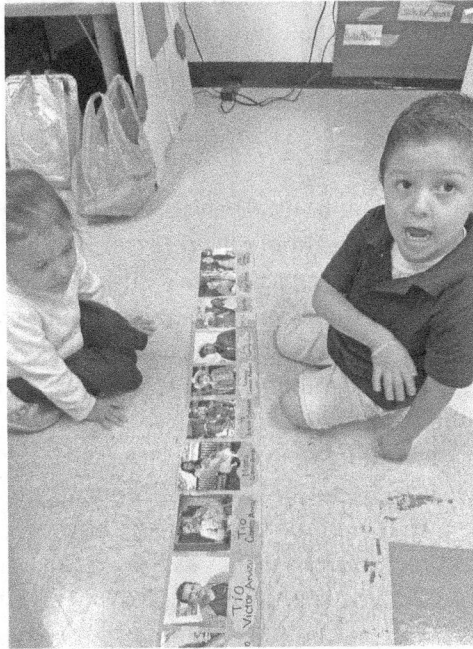

**Figure 4.4. Drawing pictures and writing a personal story.**

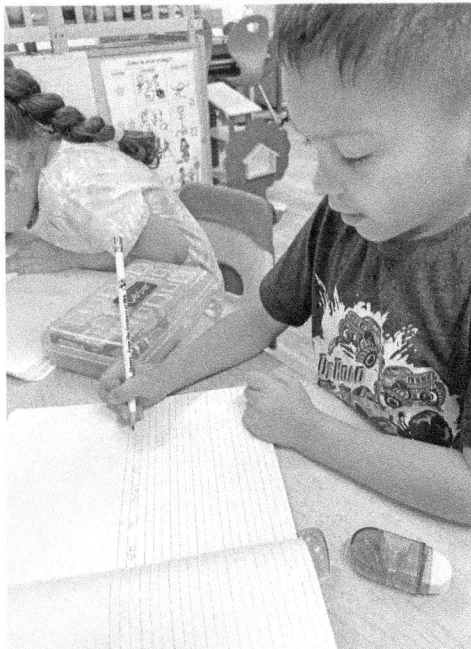

content both accessible and personally relevant. They enhance children's understanding of the world, build empathy, and, crucially, support the development of multilingualism and multiliteracies.

**TRY THIS!**

1. Read the bilingual book *René Has Two Last Names* by René Colato Laínez (2009). Preschool teachers can invite families to write their last names on a large index card. During Circle Time, have children discuss their family's last names and who they represent. Kindergarten teachers can have children draw their family tree on a large canvas and identify their family members just like René does in the story.
2. Read the bilingual book *Alfredito flies home/Alfredito regresa volando a su casa* (Argueta, 2007). Use Chatterpix, a free mobile application, to create animated talking pictures. Children can take or use a photo and record their voices as they create their own stories.
3. Read *Areli Is a Dreamer* (Morales, 2021). Have the children create a "Dream Wall" where they can draw or write about their dreams and aspirations. Discuss the importance of resilience and the idea that everyone has the right to dream and achieve their goals.

## CHAPTER 5

# Culturally Sustaining Interactive Read-Alouds as a Social Justice Practice for Developing Students' Vocabulary and Language

*Laura Cardona Berrio and María G. Leija*

Culturally sustaining pedagogies . . . *Pues mi definición para esto es tratar de invitar a todas las culturas al salón. Welcoming their own identities, que ellos se sientan apreciados* . . . (Well, my definition for this is to try to invite all cultures into the room. Welcoming their own identities, making them feel appreciated . . .)

—Ms. Giménez, pre-K dual-language teacher

## Chapter Objectives

1. Define and Examine culturally sustaining pedagogies and practices.
2. Examine the benefits of interactive read-alouds as a literacy tool for engaging young children in social justice discussions.
3. Explore a research snapshot of a culturally sustaining interactive read-aloud as a tool to examine social justice issues while developing students' vocabulary and language.
4. Share recommended children's literature to explore skin tone and diversity with young children.

As the demographics of our student population continue to shift, the number of students of color we serve continues to increase. In 2022, public school students of color enrolled in pre-K through 12th grade comprised more than 27 million Latinx, Black, Asian, American Indian, Pacific

Islander, and/or bi/multiracial students (Irwin et al., 2024). Unfortunately, the lack of attention to opportunity gaps (such as school funding, curriculum, teacher quality, etc.) continues to negatively affect the academic performance of many students of color (Milner, 2021). Researchers have noted the importance of providing students of color with a rigorous and culturally relevant/sustaining curriculum that enhances their learning experience and supports them in thriving academically (Leija & Ramírez, 2023; Muhammad, 2020).

In this chapter, we first explore culturally sustaining pedagogies (CSPs) as educational practices that center the assets young children bring to the classroom (Paris, 2021). Secondly, we discuss the benefits of interactive read-alouds and the use of culturally sustaining interactive read-alouds in early childhood classrooms. We then examine a research snapshot highlighting a preschool teacher's implementation of CSPs to discuss the concept of skin color with her young emergent bilingual students. Finally, we provide a curated list of children's picture books to facilitate discussions about diversity and skin tone, along with a mentor text approach.

## CULTURALLY SUSTAINING PEDAGOGIES

The term CSPs was coined by Paris (2012), who built on the work of seminal scholars in asset-based theories such as *funds of knowledge* (Moll & González, 1994), *third space* (Gutiérrez, 2008), and *culturally relevant pedagogy* (e.g., Ladson-Billings, 1995). CSPs invite educators to work with students to discuss issues of power and decentering whiteness to sustain their languages, literacies, and cultures.

### Key Features of Culturally Sustaining Pedagogies

Culturally sustaining pedagogies and practices have four standard features:

1. critically centering the dynamic languages, knowledge, and cultural practices of minoritized communities in diverse learning settings;
2. building trustful relationships with families, students, and elders as consultants and collaborators in the educational process;
3. creating healthy and reciprocal relationships with the land, its communities, students, and communities in general; and
4. challenging hegemonic notions by turning the inward gaze around dominant narratives of minoritized communities (Paris, 2021).

Since Paris coined the term *culturally sustaining pedagogies* in 2012, scholars and early childhood educators have integrated and extended its standard features into literacy practices in early childhood classrooms (Cardona Berrio & Arreguín, 2023; Clark, 2020; Edyburn et al., 2019). Instructional practices centered on emergent bilingual children's linguistic repertoires and cultures have also been identified. Edyburn et al. (2019) revealed outstanding practices to sustain preschool Latinx emergent bilingual children's bilingualism and academic achievement by implementing children's native language to support language development, vocabulary, and academic concepts. Clark (2020) documented the integration of the dynamic linguistic repertoires of young Spanish-English emergent bilingual children in a 2nd-grade classroom during class discussions of culturally relevant picture books in a one-way immersion program. Integrating CSPs and practices in early childhood settings, such as centering minoritized children's linguistic repertoires, is essential to address social justice issues in education, considering that young Latinx children and their families bring valuable knowledge and experiences to the classrooms.

## INTERACTIVE READ-ALOUDS

Interactive read-alouds are a common literacy practice in early childhood classrooms (Sipe, 2002) that foster dialogue between the teacher and students. Through interactive read-alouds, early childhood teachers strategically use picture books to spark meaningful conversations, making the read-aloud experience more engaging and enriching for all learners (McClure & Fullerton, 2017). Interactive read-alouds are culturally sustaining for young children when teachers intentionally select diverse books that reflect the experiences and identities of children in the classroom. Additionally, when teachers encourage children to share personal connections to the text and incorporate culturally relevant language and practices into the reading experience, children can connect to the characters and themes on a deeper personal level (Helbig & Piazza, 2020).

Interactive read-alouds also promote phonological development (phonemic awareness and phonics) (Venegas & Guanzon, 2023), as well as the development of expressive language and vocabulary. They invite children to draw on their background knowledge through social interactions (Hisrich & McCaffrey, 2021) and support children's collective meaning-making, reading comprehension through inference-making strategies, visual literacy, and motivation, due to their child-centered nature (DeJulio et al., 2022; Shimek, 2024). Other benefits include the development of academic language in content areas such as science and social studies, inferential thinking, opportunities to explore how print works, and argumentative writing development (Cabell et al., 2019).

Interactive read-alouds support gains in semantic and vocabulary knowledge of emergent bilingual children when combined with high family engagement in 3-year-old Spanish–English emergent bilingual children (August et al., 2024). Emergent bilingual children engage more actively with interactive read-alouds of culturally relevant picture books in which they share their knowledge about word meaning, pronunciation, and vocabulary in context (Christ & Cho, 2023). They also engage in meaningful discussions of multilingual books in which they share their cultural background knowledge when the discussions foster the use of their linguistic repertoires (e.g., Clark, 2020; Osorio, 2020).

Interactive read-alouds provide meaningful opportunities for young children's engagement in discussions around sociopolitical issues, such as unfairness, power imbalances, gender nonconformity, the lack of multiple perspectives, diversity, and exploring alternatives to transform unjust circumstances (Johnson et al., 2025; Lara & Leija, 2014; Wild, 2023b). For instance, Nguyen (2022) investigated the interactive read-alouds of antibias-themed picture books and found that young children can engage in thoughtful conversations around issues of racism, homophobia, white privilege, sexism, gender nonconformity, and stereotypes. The read-aloud of picture books about racial issues supports young children's reflection, empathy, and value of our pluralistic society (e.g., Fontanella-Nothom, 2019). We agree with Wild (2023a) in her assertion that read-alouds for social justice purposes are essential and we embrace diversity as a critical component of our society.

## ENGAGING STUDENTS IN A CULTURALLY SUSTAINING INTERACTIVE READ-ALOUD

In this section, we present a snapshot of research from a more extensive qualitative case study (Stake, 1995). The study focused on Ms. Giménez, a Latina Pre-K teacher, interactively reading aloud a culturally sustaining picture book about skin tones and cultural diversity to her emergent bilingual Latinx students.

Ms. Giménez taught in a prekindergarten Spanish-English 80/20 two-way dual-language immersion (TWDI) program in South Central Texas, where most of her students were of Latinx descent. There were 18 students in the prekindergarten classroom. Most students spoke Spanish at home and shared a Mexican American cultural background, except one student from an Indian American background. Twelve children were native Spanish speakers, and six were native English speakers. Ms. Giménez was born in Texas and grew up surrounded by the rich Mexican culture of her parents, who were born in Mexico. At the time of the study, she had taught prekindergarten for 5 years and was in the first year of implementing the Interdisciplinary Biliteracy Sequence (IBS) (Alanís et al., 2021; Arreguín et al., 2023). The approach entails developing oracy through three phases related to thematic units of study: (1) a sensory-based experience, (2) a writing experience, and (3) an interactive read-aloud. The elementary school's goals are global citizenship, biliteracy, and high metalinguistic skills. The data presented in this chapter stems from one of the interactive read-aloud observations.

### Goals of Two-Way Dual-Language Programs

Two-way dual-language programs attempt to integrate equal numbers of native speakers of the target languages in the classroom, and both languages are implemented for instructional purposes (Baker & Wright, 2021).

## DEVELOPING SOCIAL JUSTICE THROUGH DISCUSSIONS ABOUT SKIN TONES

Early childhood education typically centers on picture books with white main characters or animal characters and, therefore, does not allow for diverse students to see themselves positively reflected (Leija et al., 2023). Nguyen (2022) found that early childhood educators often ignore issues of race, arguing that young children are too young or innocent to understand and discuss issues of race and injustice. Research, however, has demonstrated that young children can recognize and engage with social justice issues such as racism, and can actively participate as advocates (Kesler et al., 2020). Ms. Giménez saw the value of critical discussions with her young learners. For this lesson, she led her students in a discussion about skin tone as she implemented the three phases of the IBS sequence (see Chapter 3 for additional activities on skin tone).

For Phase 1, Ms. Giménez had her students create self-portrait paintings as their sensory experience. She carefully guided each student to observe their skin tone and mix paint colors to match their skin tone. During Phase 2 (see Figure 5.1), Ms. Giménez invited students to write "Este soy yo" (this is me) and draw their self-portrait. The read-aloud for Phase 3 was the big book *Felices en Nuestra Piel* (Happy in Our Skin) (Manushkin, 2018). The

**Figure 5.1. Students' independent drawings.**

book portrays racially and ethnically diverse families sharing various city spaces, such as the park, a family home, and a swimming pool. *Happy in Our Skin* emphasizes different skin tones through rhymes and highlights the characteristics of the skin as an organ of the body that makes us unique, celebrating diversity. The read-aloud was connected to the curricular theme "My Body" and children's experiences in Phase 1 and 2 of the IBS.

An essential component of culturally sustaining practices is creating educational experiences in which the students learn that who they are and where they came from have value in the classroom, community, and society (e.g., Ladson-Billings, 1995). Self-consciousness, or the ability to know and perceive oneself in relation to others, develops during early childhood, as early as the first 18 months of life (Rochat, 2024). Through the authentic self-portrait paintings, students developed positive racial identities as they mixed the color of their skin tone, illustrated their faces with a smile, and identified themselves through their writing. The art and writing activity highlights the importance of addressing the topic of skin tones as a matter of social justice with young children, considering that young children's racial backgrounds are an essential part of their developing identities.

## Developing Students' Vocabulary Knowledge

In Phase 3 of the IBS, Ms. Giménez conducted an interactive read-aloud that supported her young children in discussing skin tones by reading the big book *Felices en nuestra piel* (*Happy in Our Skin*) (Manushkin, 2018).

The book portrays diverse families (including mixed-race families) and children with various skin tones having fun and spending time together. The book's vocabulary is explicit about the variations of skin appearance, such as freckles, birthmarks, dimples, and the characters' different skin tones. Ms. Giménez began the conversation by reading aloud the book's title and then paused to engage her students in discussing the concept of skin (see Figure 5.2).

> *Ms. Giménez: Muy bien, vamos a leer el título. El título dice, "Felices en nuestra piel". ¿Qué es piel?* (Okay, let us read the title. The title says, Happy in Our Skin. What is skin?)
> *Vivian: El color.* (The color.)
> *Rafael: El cuerpo.* (The body.)
> *Ms. Giménez: ¿Qué es piel? Enséñame dónde está su piel.* (What is skin? Show me where your skin is.)
> *Victoria*: *Aquí* [pointing to her hand]. (Here.)
> *Ms. Giménez: Aquí* [touching her hand], *muy bien* [touching her hand and forearm], *todo esto es nuestra piel.* (Here, very well, all this is our skin.)
> *Adriana*: *La cara.* (The face.)
> *Ms. Giménez: La piel que protege las partes de nuestro cuerpo. ¿Verdad que sí?* (The skin that protects our body parts. Isn't that right?)

**Figure 5.2. Reading and discussing the book's title.**

Ms. Giménez engaged the students in a semantic conversation about the vocabulary word, skin. When she asked, *"¿Qué es piel? Enséñame dónde está su piel"* ("What is skin? Show me where your skin is"), she invited students to connect the vocabulary word to their bodies by pointing to their skin. She mimicked their behavior by pointing to different parts of her body (hand and forearm). Ms. Giménez also noted one purpose of the skin, *"La piel que protege las partes de nuestro cuerpo"* ("The skin that protects our body parts"). As children touched and looked at their skin, Ms. Giménez moved children from a concrete object (skin) to an abstract concept with a discussion of skin and its primary function (Alanís et al., 2021; Arreguín et al., 2023).

### Highlighting Skin Tone Diversity

In addition to developing students' vocabulary knowledge, Ms. Giménez also supported the development of students' language while aiding them in developing an awareness of skin tone diversity within families. As she continued reading aloud, she paused at the illustration (Figure 5.3) of a nuclear multiracial family lying down at a city park admiring their newborn baby with their toddler and a young elementary-aged child.

In the following excerpt, Ms. Giménez drew students' attention to the diverse skin tones of the illustrated multiracial family.

> *Ms. Giménez: ¿Qué es lo que vemos aquí* [referring to the illustration] *en esta parte del cuento?* (What do we see here, in this part of the story?)

**Figure 5.3. Reviewing the illustrations.**

*Estudiantes: Las bebes.* (The babies.)

*Victoria: Las están acostando y les están haciendo cosquillas.* (They are lying them down and they are tickling them.)

*Ms. Giménez: ¿Le están haciendo cosquillitas? Okay, y mira la piel de las personas, ¿son diferentes o son iguales?* (Are they tickling them? Okay, and look at people's skin, are they different or are they the same?)

*Estudiantes: Son diferentes.* (They are different.)

*Ms. Giménez: Son diferentes* [referring to the characters in the illustration]. *Quizá ellos son parte de diferentes culturas, por eso es que a lo mejor tienen diferente tono de piel. Aquí vemos a esta mujer que tiene tono de piel cremita* [pointing to the woman with creamy skin tone]. *Ellos son más cafecitos* [referring to the other characters in the illustration]. *Él bebe también.* (They are different. Maybe they are part of different cultures, which is why they may have different skin tones. Here, we see this woman who has a creamy skin tone. They are more brown. The baby too.)

Ms. Giménez invited her students to pay close attention to the illustrations' details (characters and diverse skin tones). She asked the students to compare and contrast the illustrated characters, "*. . . mira la piel de las personas, ¿son diferentes o son iguales?* (". . . look at people's skin, are they different or are they the same?"), to which the engaged students enthusiastically agreed that the skin tones were different. Ms. Giménez took them one step further and modeled the literacy strategy of inferring from the illustration, "*Quizá ellos son parte de diferentes culturas, por eso es que a lo mejor tienen diferente tono de piel. Aquí vemos a esta mujer que tiene tono de piel cremita*" ("They are different. Maybe they are part of different cultures, which is why they may have different skin tones. Here, we see this woman who has a creamy skin tone"). She named and contrasted the multiple skin tones that were visibly present in the illustration (creamy and more brown).

Through the discussion, Ms. Giménez augmented children's vocabulary (e.g., tono, cremita) and modeled several literacy strategies: reading the illustration, inferring, and comparing and contrasting. Drawing attention to the diverse skin tones, she amplified the author's intended message that we should each be "happy in our skin." She centered communities of color (Paris, 2021) in her pedagogical practice, underlying racial diversity as the norm in our society. She drew attention to the happy multiracial family spending time together at the park and pointed out that the family was tickling the baby during a joyful family outing. By drawing attention to specific elements within the illustrations, the discussion enhances the positive portrayal of racial identities presented in the book, allowing children to connect to the characters and their actions.

In addition, throughout the unit, she provided materials that reflected students' racial backgrounds and resembled their skin tones, such as coloring pencils, dolls with different skin tones, and fiction and nonfiction books that provided scientific explanations for different skin tones. In a later unit, she provided picture books and guided discussion about famous U.S. Latinx (e.g., José Hernández) and Black (e.g., Dr. Martin Luther King Jr.) figures.

We consider these interactions during the interactive read-aloud a culturally sustaining literacy practice because even though Ms. Giménez was reading the book for the first time, she intentionally invited her students to notice the different skin tones portrayed in the illustration, challenging colorblind approaches in early childhood education. During the read-aloud, Ms. Giménez intentionally modeled vocabulary and provided students with opportunities to develop language as they discussed the meaning of the word *skin*, different skin tones, and cultures. Children saw themselves reflected in the stories they read, affirming their own identities and experiences.

## CHILDREN'S LITERATURE RECOMMENDATIONS: DISCUSSING SKIN TONE WITH YOUNG STUDENTS

Interactive read-alouds support teachers in sustaining children's multiple identities, literacies, cultures, and linguistic repertoires. Exposure to and interaction with children's literature that offers non-stereotypical portrayals of historically minoritized communities sustains cultural pluralism in our society and supports life-affirming discussions around students' race(s), language(s), and culture(s). We invite early childhood educators to participate in interactive read-alouds that positively showcase racially diverse communities and recognize the impacts of structural racism on young children's lives. We recommend using children's literature to facilitate discussions about race and skin tone with young learners, regardless of their ethnic identity.

In Table 5.1, we provide a list of picture books that engage young children in discussions about race and skin tone. The books provide opportunities for children to develop language by discussing questions, making connections, and sharing observations about the illustrations. They also help children develop vocabulary (e.g., melanin, skin tone, identity) and an awareness of socially constructed concepts (e.g., white privilege, race, racism) while supporting the development of positive racial identities.

Table 5.1 also includes several open-ended questions to elicit conversation about each book. The questions are designed to draw attention to

**Table 5.1. Children's Literature to Engage in Conversations Around Issues of Race and Skin Tone**

| Title & Author | Ethnic Representation and/or Topic | Summary | Discussion Questions |
|---|---|---|---|
| *I Am Brown* (Banker, 2020) | Brown children's positive racial identities. | The book celebrates Brown children, highlighting their beauty, talents, and intelligence. | Where are the Brown children from? What do you notice about their neighborhood? Is it similar to yours? <br><br> What languages do the Brown children speak? Do you speak any of those languages? <br><br> How can we describe the Brown children in the story? <br><br> How can we describe the Brown children that we know? |
| *Race Cars* (Devenny, 2021) | Black, white, and white privilege. | Through the story of a white and a black car who are best friends, the author explores issues of white privilege and supports young children in developing positive racial identities and recognizing unfairness. | Have you experienced something similar to what happened to Chase (the black race car) and Ace (the white race car)? If yes, what happened? <br><br> Think about your best friend. What are some of the similarities and differences between you and your friend? <br><br> Why do you think the organizers of the race only wanted the white cars to win? What could they do to be fair? |
| *Skin Like Mine* (Perry, 2016) | The development of young children's positive racial identities. | The book narrates the story of two Brown children who love their skin tone and conveys that skin tone should not be an obstacle to building friendships. | Let's talk about the various skin tones we have in our class. Turn and talk to your partner. Describe your skin tone. <br><br> What do you think the author meant by "color should never keep two people from being close"? <br><br> I am [share you racial identity] and my skin is ([share your skin tone]. I love having friends with different skin tones. How might it feel when a friend tells you that you cannot play with them because of your skin tone? |

*(continued)*

**Table 5.1.** (continued)

| Title & Author | Ethnic Representation and/or Topic | Summary | Discussion Questions |
|---|---|---|---|
| *Our Skin: A First Conversation About Race* (Madison & Ralli, 2021) | Ethnoracially diverse children, race, and racism. | The book portrays ethnoracially diverse children and families and is explicit about young children noticing different skin colors. It also explains race and racism and how it is present in young children's lives, giving a clear message that racism hurts and is always unfair. | What skin tones do we have in our classroom? Can you tell how smart a friend is by looking at their skin tone? Please explain your answer. |
| *M is for Melanin* (Rose, 2019) | Black children, positive racial identity, and the alphabet. | This alphabet book describes different positive aspects of the Black culture and race for each letter of the alphabet. | What is Black girl magic and Black boy joy? Why do you think we have melanin in our skin? Which was your favorite letter and why? |

some of the book's characters, connect to students' lived experiences, and discuss students' racial identities and socially constructed concepts. These questions highlight the importance of moving beyond the development of academic skills when discussing skin tone. They encourage meaningful conversations about racial diversity and acknowledge social justice issues that affect children's lives.

## CLOSING REFLECTIONS

An essential component of culturally sustaining pedagogies is to sustain students' cultural backgrounds and linguistic repertoires in educational settings (Paris, 2012; Paris & Alim, 2017). Young children's racial backgrounds are a critical component of their identities. Young children notice the racial, linguistic, and cultural diversity in their homes, schools, local and national communities. One way to center racially, culturally, and linguistically diverse communities in the curriculum is to expose young children to vocabulary representing different cultures during interactive read-alouds, as Ms. Giménez did when exposing her students to vocabulary to talk about different skin tones. Teachers may feel uncomfortable discussing issues of race, discrimination, and racism with young children, yet these aspects influence their self-concept and identity. Early childhood educators who are willing to commit to the lifelong journey of being culturally sustaining teachers and advocates must critically reflect on their own biases and prejudices, analyze the source of their discomfort regarding these topics, and take action to engage in interactive read-alouds that will challenge systemic oppressions and encourage their young learners to be social justice advocates (Wild, 2023b).

Strategies for engaging in conversations about social justice issues involve using diverse literature with young children while centering their linguistic repertoires and background knowledge. These strategies include opening spaces for translanguaging or the fluid use of young children's linguistic repertoires during conversations about social justice (Johnson et al., 2025). Early childhood teachers can support children's well-being and academic success by engaging in interactive read-alouds featuring racial diversity and social justice themes aligned with learning standards and goals.

## TRY THIS!

1. Select mentor texts to examine the author's craft (Culham, 2016). Repeated interactive read-alouds provide opportunities for students to absorb important details and long-term understanding of the topic (McGee & Schickedanz, 2017). Use the mentor texts to scaffold children's understanding of complex issues.

2. Try the mentor text approach with *M Is for Melanin* (Rose, 2019). After reading aloud the alphabet book, invite the class to analyze the author's craft and then guide students in co-authoring their very own alphabet book about skin tone.

3. Explore We Need Diverse Books (https://diversebooks.org/) for books related to skin tone and racial diversity.

## CHAPTER 6

# Picture Books, Families, and Multimodal Possibilities for Social Awareness

*Isauro M. Escamilla*

### Chapter Objectives

1. Understand why some children's books on immigration, cultural roots, or neighborhood history are banned
2. Recognize and value diversity in classroom and school communities
3. Explore innovative ideas for teacher–family partnerships
4. Strengthen home–school connections by involving families in storytelling
5. Integrate families' journeys through storytelling, drawings, and writing in the home language

Reading is more than just decoding words on a page—it is a pathway to conversation, discovery, and connection. For preschool and kindergarten children, picture books offer a rich opportunity to engage with stories that spark their curiosity, reflect their experiences, and introduce them to new perspectives. Families play a vital role in this process by reading with their children and encouraging dialogue, storytelling, and exploring themes that matter to them and their communities.

This chapter explores how families and educators can collaborate to support young children's literary journeys, drawing from research on family engagement and children's knowledge-building. Through shared reading experiences, discussions, and meaningful interactions with picture books, children develop early literacy skills while deepening their understanding of the world around them. Readers will discover practical ways to foster partnerships between teachers and families, creating a supportive environment where children can experience the joy of reading and storytelling.

## THEORETICAL APPROACHES TO USING CULTURALLY RELEVANT CHILDREN'S LITERATURE

Children's picture books can empower children of all ages to embrace their full complexity and cultural richness by telling stories about survival, heritage, and identity. Using culturally relevant children's literature to promote diversity, equity, and inclusion requires both a thoughtful, theory-driven approach and research-backed strategies based on educational principles such as critical literacy (Freire, 1970), culturally responsive teaching (Gay, 2018), funds of knowledge (Moll et al., 1992), and funds of identity (Esteban-Guitart & Moll, 2014). See Appendix B for a list of theory-driven approaches for the integration of culturally relevant children's picture books.

In today's diverse society, it is particularly important to uplift stories that represent a wide range of voices, especially those from communities that are often overlooked. In this chapter, I highlight a picture book author who offers his perspectives on the significance of promoting inclusive narratives and ensuring that children encounter books that reflect their own lives as well as the experiences of others. By embracing stories from different cultural and social backgrounds, families and educators can help children develop a love for stories, reading, and writing that is both meaningful and empowering.

One of the authors of children's picture books discussed in this chapter is the renowned writer and poet laureate Jorge Argueta, with whom I sat down in his cozy Luna's Press office and bookstore in the Mission District of San Francisco, surrounded by many of the books often seen on shelves in preschool classrooms, elementary schools, and the children's section in neighborhood libraries around the country. I spoke with Mr. Argueta regarding his opinion on challenged and banned children's books in K–12 school communities and even public libraries from California to New York and from Florida to Washington State.

One of my own picture books for children, *A Movie in my Pillow/Una película en mi almohada* [Argueta, 2007] was recently challenged because the main character is an immigrant, a young child from Central America who through a series of illustrated poems, reminisces about the important things he left back home: his first bicycle, Toki his talkative parrot, and something even more precious, his grandma, who used to talk with trees, animals and mountains in Nahuatl, her and her ancestors' native language. In several of my books I speak about the topic of immigration in Latin communities in the United States. Stories by Hispanic and Black authors have recently been "discovered" by the publishing industry and more needs to be done to promote those stories as well as those of Indigenous heritage. Those stories have not been sufficiently exposed. Stories by Hispanic, Black, and Indigenous authors in children's picture books are important because they represent who we are, where we come from, and where we want to go. There will always be an audience for children's picture books that tell our origins and how we continue to survive and thrive despite challenges our communities encounter along the way. The main message is that we feel proud of being ourselves in our whole complexity.

Jorge Argueta's interview excerpt highlights the ongoing challenges of integrating diverse children's literature into U.S. schools, particularly books that center immigrant, Latinx, Black, and Indigenous narratives. His concern about book challenges and bans in schools and libraries reflects broader debates on what is deemed "appropriate" for young readers.

A key point in Argueta's argument is that banning books like *A Movie in My Pillow/Una película en mi almohada* (2007) or *Dreamers/Soñadores* (Morales, 2018) often stems from the presence of themes such as immigration and cultural heritage rather than any specific content. The rejection of these narratives signals a resistance to stories that reflect the realities of marginalized communities, reinforcing a limited perspective on what children's literature should include. Argueta challenges this exclusion by asserting that these stories are essential for children to see themselves represented, to understand their cultural roots, and to feel a sense of pride in their identity. Moreover, he critiques the publishing industry's slow recognition of Latinx, Black, and Indigenous voices. While progress has been made in elevating these perspectives, Argueta argues that they remain underrepresented. His call for more exposure of these stories aligns with ongoing efforts in education and publishing to diversify children's literature.

## REPRESENTATION, IDENTITY, AND CULTURALLY RELEVANT CHILDREN'S BOOKS

Research in early childhood education emphasizes that when children see themselves reflected in books, they develop a stronger sense of self-worth and belonging (Zirkel & Johnson, 2016). Argueta's perspective and his books highlight the importance of Latinx, Black, and Indigenous stories and counter the dominant cultural narratives that marginalize the voices of communities of color. His call for increased visibility of these narratives aligns with Rudine Sims Bishop's (1990) concept of books as "mirrors, windows, and sliding glass doors," which argues that children need literature that reflects their experiences (mirrors), introduces them to others' experiences (windows), and allows them to step into new perspectives (sliding glass doors).

## Culturally Responsive Teaching and Family Engagement

Argueta's critique also resonates with culturally responsive education, which seeks to affirm students' cultural identities in the learning process. Families play a crucial role in this approach, as shared storytelling traditions—such as those found in Latinx and Indigenous cultures—are integral to passing down knowledge and values. When books like *Una película en mi almohada* (Argueta, 2007) are challenged or banned, it not only restricts access to diverse rich narratives but also severs a potential bridge between home cultures and what children learn at school.

Argueta's reflections remind us that book bans often reflect broader societal anxieties rather than genuine concerns about age-appropriate content. The fear of discussing immigration, racial identity, or cultural traditions in children's books is often rooted in political debates over diversity and inclusion. However, suppressing these narratives does not erase the realities of children who live them daily. Instead, it risks silencing their voices and limiting opportunities for cross-cultural understanding.

At its core, Argueta's message of resilience and affirmation is a call to action to promote and defend literature that reflects the richness of diverse communities across America. By embracing stories of people and communities overcoming adversity, migrating to new places in search of a future, and building stronger identities, educators and families can empower children to take pride in who they are, where they come from, and the journeys that shape them. Furthermore, Argueta's message of heritage, resilience, and affirmation can be traced back to the characters in some of his many bilingual children's picture books, particularly within marginalized communities in the United States. His works empower young readers to embrace their full complexity and cultural richness. Here, I introduce four picture books that I have used with my own Spanish/English bilingual preschoolers.

*A Movie in My Pillow/Una película en mi almohada (Argueta, 2007)*. This collection of poems draws from Argueta's own experiences as a child emigrating from El Salvador to San Francisco, California. Through vivid poetry, young Jorguito reminisces about his homeland and navigates the challenges of adapting to a new environment, highlighting the resilience inherent in the immigrant journey. The pictures by Elizabeth Gómez complement the story through a tapestry of blue, green, and orange clothing and background scenes.

***Xochitl and the Flowers/Xóchitl, la niña de las flores (2013)***. Based on actual events, this story follows Xochitl, a young girl who moves with her family from El Salvador to the Mission District of San Francisco. Together, they transform their new home into a vibrant flower shop, symbolizing the preservation of cultural heritage and the blossoming of new beginnings despite adversity.

***Somos como las nubes/We Are Like the Clouds (2016)***. This poignant collection of poems captures the voices of young migrants journeying north from Central America. Argueta sensitively portrays their hopes, fears, and dreams, emphasizing the strength and determination required to seek a better life while honoring one's roots.

***Talking with Mother Earth/Hablando con madre tierra (2006)***. In this collection, Argueta delves into his indigenous heritage, sharing bilingual poems that reflect a deep connection to nature and self-acceptance. Honest, moving, and raw, these powerful poems explore a young Indigenous boy's connection to Mother Earth and how he is healed from the terrible wounds of racism he has endured. The boy, Tetl, has learned from his grandmother about the spirituality of his ancestors, about how they viewed the earth as alive with sacred meaning. This helps Tetl move from doubt and fear, provoked by the taunts of other children, to self-acceptance, inner strength, and a discovery of his inner strength and love for nature.

> By embracing stories of people and communities overcoming adversity, migrating to new places in search of a future, and building stronger identities, educators and families can empower children to take pride in who they are, where they come from, and the journeys that shape them.

Jorge Argueta's picture books not only tell stories of survival and identity but also serve as affirmations of cultural pride, offering young readers mirrors reflecting their own experiences and windows into the lives of others. Through Argueta's verses and stories, children are encouraged to embrace their identities and find strength in their own cultural backgrounds. Argueta believes children's books can empower young readers by affirming their identities, celebrating their cultural heritage, and providing a space to validate their experiences and emotions.

All of Argueta's children's picture books are rooted in five core values.

**Representation and Identity Affirmation.** Argueta emphasizes that when children see themselves, their families, and their communities in books, they feel seen and valued. Many children from immigrant and marginalized backgrounds rarely encounter stories that reflect their realities, making them feel invisible. By writing books that feature Latinx, Indigenous, and immigrant children, he helps young readers embrace their full complexity—acknowledging both the struggles and joys of their identities.

**Resilience Through Storytelling.** His books often highlight the resilience of children and their families, particularly in the face of displacement, migration, and cultural adaptation. Stories like *Somos como las nubes/We Are Like the Clouds* (Argueta, 2016) give voice to young migrants, showing their fears, hopes, and determination. This allows children to see their own strength reflected back at them, reinforcing the message that their struggles do not define them, but rather contribute to their resilience.

**Cultural Heritage as Strength.** Argueta's books celebrate Indigenous traditions, languages, and ways of understanding the world, as seen in *Talking with Mother Earth/Hablando con Madre Tierra* (Argueta, 2006). By incorporating Indigenous languages and customs, he gives children a sense of pride in their roots. Rather than feeling pressure to assimilate completely, young readers are encouraged to cherish their cultural heritage as a source of wisdom and strength.

**Countering Erasure and Marginalization.** Jorge Argueta also speaks to the importance of publishing more stories by Latinx, Black, and Indigenous authors, as these narratives have historically been underrepresented or excluded from mainstream children's literature. He argues that these books counteract the erasure of marginalized voices and affirm that all children's stories are worthy of being told.

**Encouraging Dialogue and Belonging.** Finally, Argueta sees literature as a bridge between generations, communities, and cultures. Books serve as a catalyst for children to talk with their families about their history, ancestors, migration experiences, and cultural roots and traditions. Through storytelling, children can navigate complex emotions and develop a deeper sense of belonging.

## REIMAGINING CHILDREN'S PICTURE BOOKS AS CATALYSTS FOR SOCIAL JUSTICE AWARENESS

Integrating picture books into early childhood education provides a unique opportunity to foster social awareness, justice, and equity. Educators can create meaningful connections between classroom learning and home experiences by actively engaging families in the exploration of picture books (López-Robertson, 2021). When educators deliberately include texts that reflect students' backgrounds, picture books offer young children a *window* into diverse cultures, identities, and social experiences (Hayes & Francis, 2024). Carefully selected books can help children develop empathy, recognize injustices, and appreciate diverse perspectives (Short, 2018). Incorporating picture books into family engagement efforts further strengthens these outcomes

> **Carefully selected books can help children develop empathy, recognize injustices, and appreciate diverse perspectives (Short, 2018).**

by ensuring that learning extends beyond the classroom. Families bring their own unique narratives, traditions, and languages, which can enhance children's understanding of the world and deepen their appreciation for diverse social realities.

## STRATEGIES FOR INCORPORATING FAMILIES' HOME LANGUAGES AND LITERACIES

To ensure inclusivity, educators can create opportunities for families to engage with picture books in their home languages through several effective strategies:

- **Bilingual Book Initiatives:** Providing picture books in multiple languages to support dual-language learners and validate linguistic diversity (for examples, see Chapter 4 of this text).
- **Family Bookmaking Projects:** Encouraging families to contribute stories, drawings, and text in their preferred language.
- **Home Language Storytelling Sessions:** Inviting family members to read aloud in their native languages, helping children develop multilingual literacy skills and cultural pride.

- **Translation Partnerships:** Collaborating with bilingual parents or community members to translate classroom books into various languages.

By implementing these approaches, educators can create a literacy-rich environment that respects and incorporates the linguistic assets of all students and their families.

## Co-creation of Artistic Products to Highlight Social Justice Themes

A particularly impactful way to deepen family engagement with picture books is through collaborative artistic projects. These projects allow children and their families to process and express social justice themes in creative ways. Some successful approaches include:

- **Classroom Murals:** Families and children work together to create visual representations of themes such as kindness, inclusion, and community.
- **Family-Illustrated Books:** Parents and children illustrate and write stories that reflect their perspectives on fairness and social equity.
- **Digital Storytelling Projects:** Families use multimedia formats (e.g., video, audio, and digital illustrations) to share their narratives and experiences (see Chapter 4 of this text).

These projects provide children with an outlet for critical thinking and emotional expression, reinforcing key social justice messages through multimodal engagement.

## Integrating Global Storytelling Traditions into Classroom Practices

Understanding and incorporating global storytelling traditions enriches classroom discussions around social justice. Educators can:

- **Research cultural storytelling practices:** Explore oral traditions and book cultures from different parts of the world.
- **Invite families to share traditional stories:** Encourage storytelling from grandparents and extended family members.
- **Use picture books from diverse global perspectives:** Select books that highlight traditions, folktales, and historical narratives from various cultures.

Teachers cultivate a more inclusive and socially aware classroom environment by recognizing and celebrating storytelling traditions. Family engagement in picture book–based learning fosters social awareness, justice, and equity by validating children's identities, embracing linguistic diversity, and amplifying the voices of families. Through culturally responsive strategies, educators can create opportunities for families to participate in meaningful classroom literacy experiences, ultimately strengthening the home–school connection. The approaches outlined in this chapter highlight the transformative power of picture books and multimodal engagement in shaping young learners' understanding of social justice and equity.

The following section explores practical strategies for linking family engagement with picture books, particularly in early childhood preschool and kindergarten settings. I use two classroom case studies to illustrate how teachers can use culturally responsive and developmentally appropriate strategies to affirm children's identities and integrate family participation into literacy activities. Additionally, I highlight strategies for incorporating home languages and literacies and engaging families in co-creating artistic products that emphasize social justice themes.

## PICTURE BOOKS AND ENGAGING FAMILIES IN CLASSROOMS—KEY EXAMPLES

### Classroom Example #1: Transitional Kindergarten

In a public transitional kindergarten classroom, Ms. Leti (teacher) and Karen (student teacher) designed a project in which children and their families co-created picture books based on their lived experiences. The process began with the teachers selecting social justice–themed picture books and facilitating classroom discussions about fairness, kindness, and equity (Table 6.1). (See Appendix C for additional books and prompts.)

After reading *Say My Name* (Ho, 2023) Ms. Leti and Karen used these two prompts in English and Spanish to engage children in a whole class discussion: (1) "Why do you think Unhei felt nervous about saying her name? / ¿Por qué creen que Unhei se sintió nerviosa al decir su nombre?" (2) "What can we do to show respect for names that sound different from ours? / ¿Qué podemos hacer para mostrar respeto a los nombres que suenan diferentes a los nuestros?". The following are some of the children's responses to prompt 1 that Karen captured in quick notes in her notebook:

**Table 6.1. Social Justice–Themed Picture Books About Fairness, Kindness, and Equity**

| | Title, Author, and Publication Date | Book Description | Class Discussion Question(s) |
|---|---|---|---|
| **Children's Books About Kindness and Empathy** | *Be Kind* by Pat Zietlow Miller (2018) | A gentle story about small acts of kindness and their big impact. | • What are some small ways we can show kindness every day?<br>• How does kindness make people feel? |
| | *A Little Spot of Kindness* by Diane Alber (2019) | A great introduction to what kindness looks like in action. | • What are some ways the "Kindness Spot" helps people in the story?<br>• Can you think of a time when you showed kindness to someone? How did it make them (and you) feel? |
| **Children's Picture Books about Equity, Inclusion, and Diversity** | *Say My Name* by Joanna Ho (2023) | Explores cultural identity and embracing one's unique name. | • Why did Unhei feel nervous about her name?<br>• How can we show respect for names that are different from our own? |
| | *Intersection Allies: We Make Room for All* by Chelsea Johnson, LaToya Council, and Carolyn Choi (2019) | A simple introduction to intersectionality for young readers. | • What does it mean to be an ally?<br>• How can we help friends who are treated unfairly? |
| **Children's Picture Books on Justice and Standing Up for Others** | *Change Sings* by Amanda Gorman, illustrated by Loren Long (2021) | A poetic call to action about making a difference. | • What does "change" mean in this story?<br>• How can kids help change the world? |
| | *Sometimes People March* by Tessa Allen (2020) | Explains protests and activism in an accessible way for young children. | • Why do people march?<br>• What are some peaceful ways people can stand up for what is right? |

"Porque su nombre era diferente" /"Because her name was different."—Julio

"She thought her classmates would make fun and laugh." / "Pensaba que los niños se iban a burlar y reír."—Marcus

"La niña era nueva en la escuela y no conocía a nadie. The girl was new at school and didn't know anyone."

"She wanted her friends to like her." / "Quería que sus compañeros la quisieran."

Ms. Leti acknowledged all the children's contributions and followed up their ideas by summarizing: "Yes, sometimes we feel nervous when people don't know our name or when it sounds new. Names are special, and it can feel hard when others don't say them right." After a brief pause she offered children the second prompt: "What can we do to show respect for names that sound different from ours? / ¿Qué podemos hacer para mostrar respeto a los nombres que suenan diferentes a los nuestros?" Children's responses:

"Podemos escuchar con cuidado." / "We can listen carefully."—Luz
   María
"Podemos tratar de decirlo bien." / "We can try to say it the right
   way."—Josie
"Podemos preguntarle cómo se dice su nombre." / "We can ask her
   how to say her name."—Raúl
"We don't laugh at names." / "No hay que reirse de los nombres."
   —Jaime
"We can say, 'That's a beautiful name!'" / "Podemos decir: '¡Qué
   nombre tan bonito!'"

Ms. Leti replied by enthusiastically saying: "Yes! Everyone's name is important. Saying someone's name correctly is one way to show love and respect. We can all practice together."

Following the classroom discussions, families were invited to be creative with their children to develop their own illustrated narratives. But how can we invite parents to be creative with their children? In this case, Ms. Leti and Karen sent a note and an email that warmly welcomed families to participate. The language of the note emphasized fun, creativity, and collaboration rather than "homework" (see Appendix E for a longer sample invitation to families):

We've been enjoying the story [Book Title] in class! We would love for your family to join in the fun by retelling the story in your own way. You can be as creative as you wish—draw, act it out, sing, or even make a short video together. The important thing is to share your ideas and voices.

Families played an integral role by contributing stories in their home languages, offering cultural insights, and guiding the artistic representation of their experiences. The project not only reinforced the importance of multilingual literacy but also showed the power of storytelling as a tool for social change. The homemade books were shared during a family literacy night, celebrating the diverse voices within the classroom and school community. Ms. Leti and Karen supported families by acknowledging different strengths and resources, so providing choices made participation more accessible:

- **Art**: Draw or paint a favorite scene.
- **Drama**: Act out the story with costumes, puppets, or toys.
- **Music**: Create a simple song or rhythm to retell the story.
- **Writing**: Dictate or write a new ending or add a new character.
- **Multimedia**: Make a short video or slideshow with family voices and photos.

### Classroom Example #2: Bilingual Kindergarten

In a public bilingual kindergarten classroom, educators implemented a family storytelling initiative using picture books centered on themes of identity and belonging. Ms. Ana Maria (teacher) and Mr. Pablo (teacher's aide) invited family members to participate by selecting books that resonated with their cultural backgrounds and reading them aloud to the class. Parents and caregivers were encouraged to share personal stories related to the themes of the books, creating a bridge between home and school literacy practices. To further deepen engagement, the teachers provided opportunities for families to contribute artifacts such as photographs, drawings, and written reflections to a class book. This collaborative book evolved into a collective narrative reflecting the classroom community's diversity and experiences. The project fostered a sense of pride and inclusivity among students by affirming each child's identity and family history.

### Classroom Example #3: Engaging Families in Storytelling

In a Spanish–English kindergarten classroom, a dedicated teacher, Miss Cruz, has developed innovative literacy activities that connect school and home while reinforcing children's identities. I describe two of these activities and explain their significance for children's learning and development.

#### Autobiographies as Personal Narratives

Miss Cruz invites children and their families to create their own autobiographies. She provides a simple template that children take home to fill with their stories; to their texts they add photographs from family albums that document key aspects of their lives. These autobiographies are then displayed throughout the classroom and school, celebrating the diversity of the students and reinforcing their sense of self and belonging.

### The Traveling Stuffed Animal Project

Another bookmaking activity involves a stuffed animal that children name and take home for a week (see Figures 6.1 and 6.2).

Families document their children's experiences with the stuffed animal through photographs—sharing meals, playing, visiting the park, going

**Figure 6.1. The adventures of Noey.**

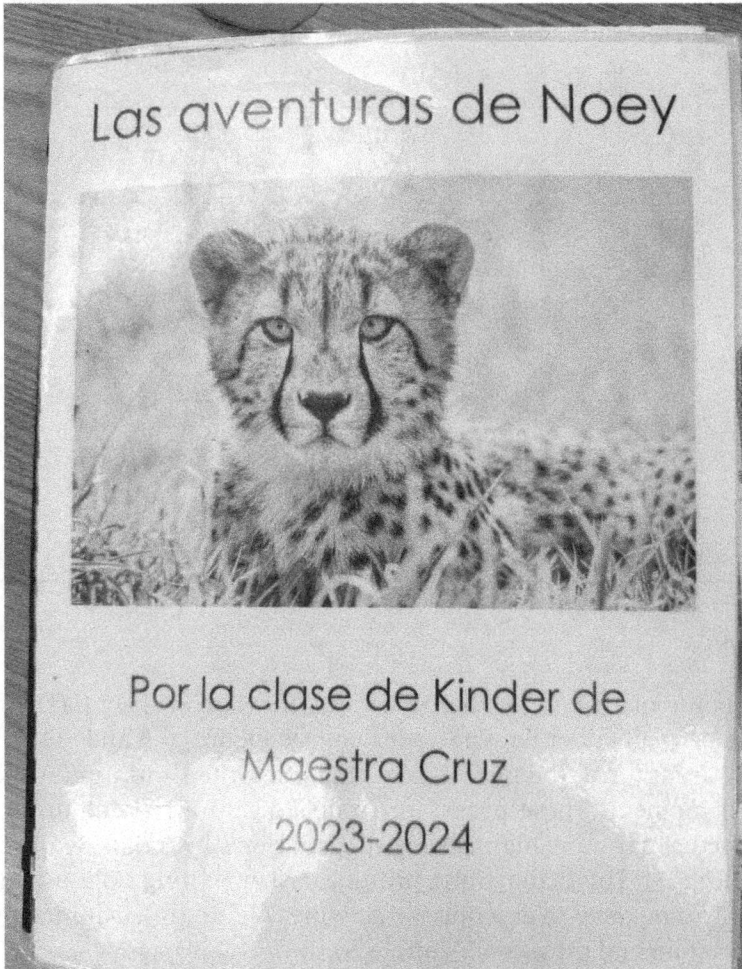

**Figure 6.2. A page from the class book showing Noey with Pardo, a family's pet.**

**Figure 6.3. Luna, the ajolote.**

shopping or relaxing at home, as was the case with Luna, the *ajolote*, a type of salamander native to Mexico (see Figures 6.3 and 6.4).

Parents print the photos, and children write short captions describing each moment. These pages are compiled into a class album, creating a collective narrative highlighting the children's lives outside of school (see Figure 6.5). This activity also promotes early writing skills as children are highly motivated to describe the activities of the stuffed animal using their developmental print (see Figure 6.6).

**Figure 6.4. Luna riding on Guero, a family's cat.**

**Figure 6.5. Each child's story is collected in a class binder.**

*Translation:* Luna met my cat *El Guero* and they became friends.

**Figure 6.6. A child's description of what they did with Luna at home.**

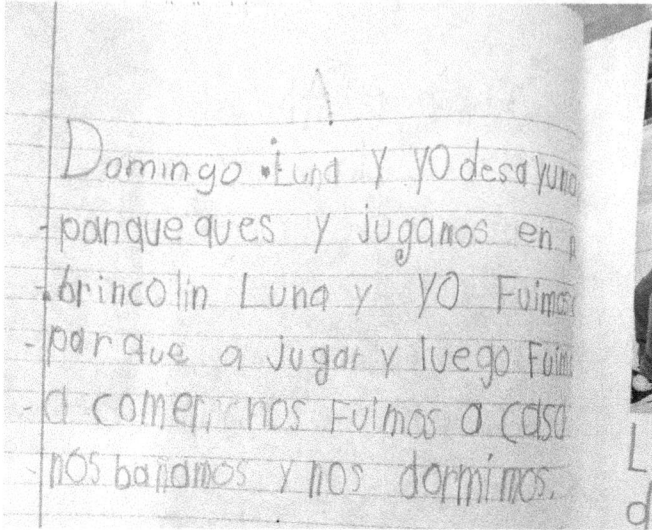

This is a journal entry written by a kindergarten child about Luna, the stuffed toy they took home for the weekend. *Translation*: Sunday. Luna and I had pancakes for breakfast, and we played in the trampoline. Luna and I went to play at the park and then we went home to eat. We showered and we went to sleep.

## Why These Approaches Matter

Miss Cruz has implemented these activities for the past 8 years because she believes literacy in kindergarten is more than just learning about letters and their sounds; it should engage children in meaningful storytelling. By incorporating children's voices and lived experiences into classroom activities, she empowers them to see themselves as authors of their own narratives. Through these activities, she fosters equity and inclusion by validating children's identities through personal storytelling. This expands the definition of literature to include children's self-made books alongside published works. In the process, she builds reciprocal relationships with families by creating a shared literacy experience where children reveal their creativity and storytelling skills.

## Rethinking Literature: Stories from Families and Communities

Miss Cruz's work challenges traditional notions of what constitutes literature. While professionally published picture books play a crucial role in literacy development, so do the stories children and families create together. These personal narratives are powerful tools for fostering identity, social awareness, and a sense of belonging. By reimagining literacy as a collective, community-driven process, educators and families can work together to nurture young readers who are not only skilled in reading and writing but also deeply aware of the diverse world around them.

## Family Literacy: Strengthening Home–School Connections

Research on family literacy highlights that when families are involved in children's reading and writing experiences, children develop stronger literacy skills and deeper connections to their learning (Moll et al., 1992). Miss Cruz's activities, such as the autobiography project and the stuffed animal storytelling, exemplify the integration of funds of knowledge—the idea that children's home experiences are valuable sources of learning (Alanís & Salinas-González, 2023).

By encouraging children to document their lives and share their stories, Miss Cruz:

- Acknowledges families as key partners in literacy development.
- Makes reading and writing relevant by connecting it to children's everyday experiences.
- Creates a bridge between school and home, ensuring that children see literacy as part of their personal and family identities.

Culturally responsive teaching (Gay, 2018) emphasizes that education should be meaningful and inclusive of students' cultural backgrounds. Miss Cruz's innovative approaches reflect this by:

- **Affirming children's identities.** The autobiographies and stuffed animal narratives celebrate the children's experiences, making them feel valued and seen.
- **Expanding the definition of literature.** She includes published books and children's creations, reinforcing the idea that their voices matter.
- **Encouraging critical thinking about equity and inclusion.** When children read and discuss books about social justice, they learn to reflect on issues that matter to them and their families. They also serve as bridges to broader social justice themes for children of all backgrounds. Teachers can use these books to compare experiences with those of other immigrant communities (e.g., Asian, African, Middle Eastern).

## FROM THEORY TO PRACTICE

Throughout this chapter, I have shared how educators can use picture books to promote social awareness, equity, and a sense of belonging for all children and their families. In this section, I showcase how early childhood teachers can use the literary works of Jorge Argueta, Yuyi Morales, and René Colato Laínez to promote cultural awareness and appreciation of Latino/a identities in their classrooms and communities. These children's book authors create stories that reflect the lived experiences, languages, and traditions of Latinx children, offering mirrors for Latinx students and windows for non-Latinx students to learn about diverse cultures. Table 6.2 shows how teachers can use these three authors' children's picture books to foster cultural pride, social justice, and community connections.

## CLOSING REFLECTIONS

Research on bilingual and emergent literacy development (García & Wei, 2014; Moll et al., 1992) underscores the importance of incorporating home languages into early reading experiences. Children do not learn languages in isolation—they build on their home linguistic practices, developing literacy in multiple languages when given authentic opportunities to engage with books in ways that reflect their lived experiences. Picture books can affirm children's identities, connect them with their families' cultural roots, and foster meaningful social interactions. When families actively engage in picture books with their children in their home languages and literacies, they help strengthen bilingual development, validate their lived experiences, and cultivate a sense of belonging in the school community and beyond. This chapter explored developmentally appropriate and culturally responsive strategies for involving families in picture book activities that honor linguistic diversity and encourage multimodal storytelling. It also provided examples from preschool and kindergarten classrooms where children, educators, and families collaboratively create picture books that incorporate home languages, family stories, photographs, and artistic expressions. These practices ensure that families are not just passive recipients of school literacy efforts but active co-creators of knowledge and culture. By incorporating these books and strategies, early childhood teachers can create inclusive, identity-affirming classrooms that honor children's multilingual and multiliteracy experiences and foster cross-cultural empathy and understanding.

**Table 6.2. Culturally Relevant Strategies and Activities**

| Author's Background | Topics to Explore | Classroom Strategies and Activities | | |
|---|---|---|---|---|
| **Jorge Argueta**, a Salvadoran author and poet, writes bilingual "Cooking Poems" that celebrate Latinx food, culture, and storytelling. His books, such as *Sopa de frijoles/ Bean Soup* provide rich descriptions of family traditions. | Promoting cultural identity through food and poetry | **Cooking and Storytelling Connections:**<br><br>Read *Sopa de frijoles/ Bean Soup* and invite families to share their own food traditions.<br><br>Have students work with their families to create their own food-related poems and illustrations.<br><br>Introduce cooking activities in the classroom. This will allow children to experience sensory learning, connect to home traditions, and build a sense of belonging. | **Exploring Migration and Identity:**<br><br>Books like *Somos como las nubes/We Are Like the Clouds* introduce children to the experiences of Central American migrant children.<br><br>Facilitate discussions on migration, homes, and families, helping children reflect on what "home" means to them. | **Bilingual Literacy Development:**<br><br>Argueta's bilingual books help children practice reading in both Spanish and English.<br><br>Invite parents or community members to read the stories in Spanish, fostering intergenerational connections. |
| **Yuyi Morales**, a Mexican American author and illustrator, creates vibrant, heartfelt stories highlighting themes of resilience, creativity, and immigrant experiences. Her books, such as *Dreamers/ Soñadores* (2018) and *Niño Wrestles the World* (2015), offer powerful messages of empowerment and cultural pride. | Celebrating immigrant experiences and creativity | **Exploring the Immigrant Experience:**<br><br>*Dreamers* tells Morales's story of coming to the United States with her child, finding a home in libraries, and embracing bilingualism.<br><br>Use this book to discuss immigration, perseverance, and the role of books in helping children feel at home in new places. | **Creative Expression through Art and Storytelling:**<br><br>Morales's books emphasize imagination and artistic expression.<br><br>Have children create illustrated books about their identities, using mixed-media art as Morales does.<br><br>Invite families to a "Storytelling Night," where children and | **Bilingual and Translanguaging Awareness:**<br><br>Highlight how Morales integrates Spanish words into her English texts.<br><br>Have children experiment with mixing languages in their own storytelling, affirming the linguistic practices of bilingual children. |

*(continued)*

**Table 6.2.** *(continued)*

| Author's Background | Topics to Explore | Classroom Strategies and Activities | | |
|---|---|---|---|---|
| | | Include "My Dream" projects, where children illustrate their aspirations and share their family's migration stories (if they are comfortable). | parents share oral traditions and personal histories. | |
| **René Colato Laínez,** a Salvadoran American author, writes stories that center bilingual, bicultural, and immigrant children in a way that validates their experiences. His books, like *Waiting for Papá* (2015) and *Mamá the Alien* (2016), address the challenges and joys of growing up in two cultures. | Uplifting bicultural and immigrant identities | Addressing Family Separation and Immigration Stories: *Waiting for Papá* (2015) tells the story of a child awaiting their father's U.S. residency approval. Create "Family Tree" projects where students explore their family backgrounds, acknowledging the complexities of migration and separation. Create a "Letters to Loved Ones" activity, where children write or draw messages to family members they miss. | Discussing Identity and Citizenship: *Mamá the Alien/ Mamá la extraterrestre* (2016) humorously explores a child's misunderstanding of immigration status. Facilitate discussions about citizenship, identity, and belonging in a developmentally appropriate way. Use role-playing activities where children act out different perspectives to develop empathy and understanding. | Encouraging Dual-Language Expression: *René Has Two Last Names* (2009) discusses naming traditions in Latinx cultures and the significance of keeping both maternal and paternal last names. Have children explore the meanings behind their own names and create name art projects. |

## TRY THIS!

1. Validate home languages in children's picture books as valuable tools for communication and learning.
2. Strengthen home–school connections by involving families in multilingual storytelling and children's picture books.

3. Promote biliteracy and translanguaging by allowing children to move fluidly between languages in storytelling, book sharing, and comprehension. Encourage families to use their full linguistic repertoire when telling stories and reading with children at home. Organize Multilingual Storytelling Nights where parents read books in Spanish, English, Indigenous or other languages. Include art projects for children and families to coauthor and co-create art and books together.

4. Develop a Classroom Library Exchange where families borrow and contribute culturally relevant books. Include books written by authors from the communities represented in the classroom.

## CHAPTER 7

# Using Child-Centered Curricular Approaches to Amplify Social Justice and Equity Content

*Iliana Alanís*

> When we acknowledge what children bring as assets, we are intentionally communicating "I see you, and you matter." There is power in being seen and celebrated.
>
> —NAEYC, 2022

## Chapter Objectives

1. Highlight how picture books can amplify classroom social justice and equity content through emergent curricula theme-based activities and project-based learning.
2. Describe how active, child-centered curricular approaches can utilize picture books to center equity and social justice in the classroom.
3. Share ideas and strategies to incorporate picture books as artifacts in dramatic play areas, early writing in personal journals, drawing and art-based projects, author studies, and theme content linked with specific picture books.

Between the ages of 3 and 5, children are actively developing their identities. This period coincides with their entry into formal schooling, where educators play a crucial role in shaping identities (Lynn & Parker, 2006). Unfortunately, schools mirror the broader societal inequities found within our society, contributing to an ongoing cycle of social reproduction. During early childhood, children develop an internalized sense of how things are in school and the broader world. Regrettably, in many early childhood contexts, racism and discrimination exist as part of the early childhood experience (Allen et al., 2021).

A strong sense of identity is vital to children's social and academic development. Although many factors contribute to this identity (families, media, peers), early childhood educators can significantly promote children's positive cultural, social, and linguistic identity development through curricula and materials. Derman-Sparks and Edwards's (2010) vision for antibias education supports children and families in creating a sense of identity and fairness and advocating for the rights of others. Through critical discussions, children build their foundational values, emerging identities, and democratic principles. When children think critically about social justice issues, they develop new possibilities for understanding and interacting with their world.

> Introducing social justice concepts at an early age helps children develop empathy and a deeper understanding of the world as they appreciate different cultures, races, and languages (Derman-Sparks et al., 2020).

Effective educators believe that young children can talk about social justice issues and develop an awareness of complex problems. They recognize that young children understand the harmful effects of inequitable practices (Sullivan, 2022; Van Ausdale & Feagin, 2002). Often, however, teachers feel unprepared for these complex discussions (Sturdivant & Alanís, 2019; Vittrup, 2016). As a result, they might ignore social justice and equity issues, minimize discussions, and implement a colorblind curriculum (Kuh et al., 2016). Without the appropriate knowledge base, early childhood educators may inadvertently contribute to oppression and discrimination (Boutte, 2008). This is compounded further by an era of censorship (ALA, 2025) and commercially bought scripted curricula (Vaughn et al., 2022) that restrict the topics from which teachers choose their focus.

These fears and restrictions notwithstanding, young children are active participants in the social construction of their worlds and are aware of social inequities at an early age (Winkler, 2009), displaying clear racial preferences and prejudices by preschool (Derman-Sparks & Ramsey, 2011; MacNevin & Berman, 2017). These preferences increase through the elementary years (Pushkin & Veness, 2017). As educators, we must acknowledge that discrimination already impacts our children's lives. They are exposed to negative messages from presidential candidates, podcasters, and comedians. Children learn from their environment and the adults they observe. They develop beliefs and attitudes about differences and may replicate society's discriminatory practices unless we challenge these biases with antiracist and antibias curricula (Derman-Sparks et al., 2020; Kendi, 2019).

This chapter shows how picture books can amplify social justice and equity content in classrooms with theme-based emergent curriculum and project-based learning. Using examples from early childhood classrooms, the chapter describes how active, child-centered curricular approaches can utilize picture books to center equity and social justice in the classroom. Lastly, this chapter presents ideas and strategies for teachers to integrate picture books into their curriculum and classroom spaces.

## USING PICTURE BOOKS TO AMPLIFY CLASSROOM SOCIAL JUSTICE AND EQUITY CONTENT

Early childhood educators are uniquely positioned to teach social justice and promote an antibias curriculum that challenges racism and prejudice while upholding respect, equity, and justice (Hawkins, 2014; Wild, 2023b). The preschool and kindergarten years shape children's understanding of their world as they develop their moral structures through sociocultural interactions with their family, culture, and society (MacNaughton & Williams, 2008; Rogoff, 2003). Research reveals that children of color who do not have a strong racial identity face greater academic challenges (Zirkel & Johnson, 2016). Research also shows that positive identity development can enhance children's overall educational success and psychological well-being (Brittian et al., 2013; Chavous et al., 2008).

Children need the time and space to talk and make sense of what they see and hear in order to understand and challenge social justice issues. Picture books can effectively initiate critical conversations and address social justice issues (Enriquez et al., 2017; Hayes & Francis, 2024; Husband, 2019; Lysaker & Sedberry, 2015; Souto-Manning, 2013). Because picture books often include themes of kindness, tolerance, acceptance of difference, and characters demonstrating courage, determination, and defiance (Short, 2018), they can contribute to children's understanding of social justice issues.

Curricular approaches like theme-based emergent curriculum and project-based learning offer active inquiry learning models to support children's cultural knowledge and lived experiences. They embrace children's experiences as critical for understanding the complex societal inequities that affect and surround them (Alvarez, 2018). These child-centered curricular approaches are significant for young learners because they

- appeal to and fulfill children's desire for agency and authentic, meaningful learning
- integrate children's culture, language, and experiences into the classroom
- support family collaboration and promote reciprocity
- challenge dominant ideology and raise critical issues
- provide teachers with windows into children's lives

These are at the core of a social justice orientation to learning and teaching (Solórzano, 1997).

## Theme-Based Instruction Through Inquiry Learning

Inquiry learning provides the space and time for children to explore and find answers to their questions about their world (Stacey, 2018). It positions children and teachers as active participants in learning and co-constructing meaning. Using inquiry connected to children's picture books is valuable for young children to learn about difference and diversity, critical thinking, and empathy (Baldwin, 2018; Hawkins, 2014; Kimura et al., 2021).

An inquiry approach to learning is facilitated through theme-based instruction that promotes meaningful learning, intrinsic motivation, and communicative competence. Thematic instruction offers optimal conditions for children because language is continually recycled throughout the unit, children are given multiple opportunities to use the new language, and they have multiple opportunities to read, discuss, and write about the concepts, language, and experiences within an authentic context (Chumdari & Budiyono, 2018).

Inquiry learning is centered around child-directed learning that prioritizes children's experiences, interests, and motivations. Here, I discuss two inquiry-based curricula that follow a thematic structure: emergent curriculum and project-based learning. I will share examples of how the topic of immigration was introduced through picture books within each. I focus on immigration because of the current sociopolitical climate, the increasing number of immigrant children, and its unique relationship to agency (resisting injustice and overcoming barriers) (Sotirovska & Kelley, 2020). Addressing immigration is vital for early childhood educators who aim to eliminate systemic disparities that perpetuate discrimination and racism (Bersh, 2013).

***Emergent Curriculum.*** Based on a Reggio Emilia philosophy of education, the emergent curriculum approach views children as capable, creative, resourceful, and collaborative (Jones & Stacey, 2018). Within an emergent curriculum, teachers adhere to state standards and guidelines but allow children's interests, thinking, and choices to determine a curricular path. Teachers build on meaningful ideas and experiences in the children's lives. Children's learning motivation increases because the teacher fosters their sense of belonging, purpose, and agency.

Although no longer in the classroom, Dr. Isauro Escamilla (the first author of this text) taught Spanish-English preschool at Las Americas in San Francisco's Mission District. His classroom included first- and second-generation immigrant families from Mexico and Central America. To identify child-initiated interests and plan emergent curriculum projects, Isauro and his colleagues listened to children's informal discussions during lunch, snack time, and outdoor play and observed their interactions.

During a project on *familias,* the children read several picture books related to family experiences. Teachers encouraged various artistic responses to the family-related texts, including drawing, construction, dramatic play, music, singing, and dancing. Children's work was liberally displayed, showcasing sketches, drawings, and paintings of their families. Teachers overheard 4-year-old Jason talking to his friend: "*El trabajo de mi papá es arreglar cosas, como las paredes y los techos de las casas viejas*" ("My dad fixes things, like walls and roofs of old houses"). He added that his mother worked in someone's home caring for a boy named Sam. Teachers encouraged Jason to share his stories and paintings about his home life and experiences. Jason and his classmates used stories to make meaning from the complex ideas they were learning about as they saw themselves represented in the curriculum through picture books (López-Robertson, 2021).

***Project-Based Learning.*** Project-based learning embraces children's interests and the immediate environment for in-depth study of a specific topic from multiple perspectives (Helm & Katz, 2010). Investigations, based on child-led conversations and inquiries, may last a few days to several months as children focus on finding answers to questions about a topic. Projects are relevant to children's lived experiences as they demonstrate their learning through drawings, discussions, and writings. When children realize that their ideas result in action, their self-esteem and agency are enhanced. The combination of inquiry and agency that project-based learning presents provides children and families with the space to explore and co-construct the stories of their choice (Alvarez, 2018).

Dr. Escamilla selected books connected to children's cultural and linguistic heritage to help them develop their bicultural and bilingual identity. For their project on *familias* the class read *A Movie in My Pillow/Una película en mi almohada* by Jorge Argueta (2007), a Salvadoran author residing in San Francisco. Isauro selected the book because the main character, Jorgíto, lives in the Mission District, like the children. One of the poems, "When we left El Salvador," resonated with 5-year-old Zahid (see Escamilla, 2023, and Chapter 8 of this text for more on Zahid's story).

Zahid shared a story about his father trying to cross the border. On a map, Zahid indicated Mexico City, where his dad started his journey to the North to reunite with his family. He highlighted where his father crossed the border and described *la frontera* (the border) as a place where "*te arrestan porque eres inmigrante*" (they arrest you because you are an immigrant). Using paintbrushes and acrylic colors, Zahid painted the dividing wall between Mexico and the United States (see Figure 7.1) and added a yellow sun on the U.S. side of the wall. He indicated that is what his dad would see on his arrival to California (see Figure 7.2).

Through his representation, Zahid reveals an understanding of the immigrant plight well beyond his 5 years of age. Several other children shared their connections with leaving loved ones behind in Mexico and Central America throughout the project. Teachers found that children developed a stronger sense of community as they discussed their shared border-crossing experiences. This exemplified children's communal knowledge, which is often excluded from the curriculum.

## THE SIGNIFICANCE OF PICTURE BOOKS FOR UNDERSTANDING SOCIAL JUSTICE ISSUES

Sharing high-quality picture books allows for critical discussions about emotion-provoking conflicts and events that may mirror those experienced by children. These critical discussions encourage children to listen to others and clarify and justify their feelings, ideas, and beliefs (Tager, 2022). They facilitate literary talks about racial, ethnic, and cultural diversity, using children's lived experiences. For example, Zaid described how he feels waiting for his dad on this side of the border and expressed his desire to be with him in Mexico when he is older. He explained his feelings and ideas about immigration and the inequitable treatment of migrants and how he perceives it based on his experiences. Children learn about dynamic human experiences through conversations as they develop oracy and literacy skills (Kim & Heyneman, 2015). Siraj-Blatchford and Sylva (2004) refer to these discussions as shared sustained thinking

**Figure 7.1. Zahid working on painting.**

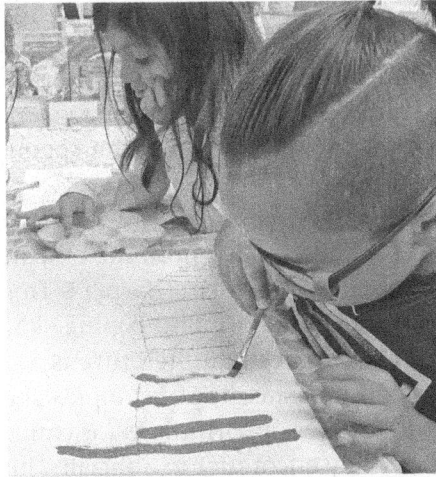

**Figure 7.2. El Muro (The Wall), Zahid's completed painting.**

characterized by sustained cognitive engagements. Discussions allow for social inclusion, intellectual engagement, and a pedagogy of listening (Dahlberg & Moss, 2005; Rinaldi, 2006), as teachers and children actively listen to others' views and understandings (Hawkins, 2014).

Too often, educators avoid discussing children's experiences with immigration and border crossing, fearing these topics may be too sensitive or controversial (Gallo & Link, 2016). However, through these examples, we hear children share their untold stories and learn various perspectives on complex situations as teachers open discussions to explore experiences and shape their attitudes on multiple issues. Picture books help children understand that their experiences are not unique, affirm their sense of identity, and help them take pride in themselves and their families (Sánchez & Landa, 2016). For instance, Jason described the reality of many immigrant Latinx families—parents working long hours, sometimes caring for other people's children, while their own children spend the day in school and after-school care.

Picture books heighten children's awareness of emotions, reinforce positive self-concepts and identity, promote empathetic behaviors toward others, and foster moral development (Harper & Trostle-Brand, 2010; Tager, 2022). This helps foster resilience and coping skills (Harper, 2016; Wild, 2023a). Bishop (1990) argues that literature is a tool for young children to help develop their understanding of complex social issues. Reading and discussing literature creates opportunities for children to critically analyze all the "differences" they encounter in a racially, linguistically, and culturally diverse world. The stories of Jason and Zahid remind us that young immigrant children learn to navigate two worlds, languages, and cultures as they live in the United States while missing their loved ones left behind. In both cases, children reclaimed and integrated critical conversations as intellectual actors through their immigration projects.

## STRATEGIES AND TIPS FOR INTEGRATING PICTURE BOOKS CONNECTED TO SOCIAL JUSTICE ISSUES

Several strategies and literacy-based activities can facilitate children's discussion, promote vocabulary development and comprehension, and enhance their cultural knowledge and understanding in meaningful ways. Here are a few strategies for you to consider:

- **Engage in the intentional curation of texts**—Consider text sets where you select titles by diverse authors on a specific topic. Search bookstores, thrift stores, and library giveaways for titles that reflect equity, diversity, and students' experiences. Talk to your librarian about ordering specific book titles. Look for winners of such awards as the Pura Belpré Award and the Tomás Rivera Mexican American Children's Book Award (Osorio, 2020). Edit books from your classroom library if they do not align with your intentions (Hayes & Francis, 2024).
- **Use literature on social justice issues in classroom read-alouds**—Read the text several times to familiarize yourself with the storyline and illustrations (Wild, 2023b). Consider how you

will use the text and the types of questions you will ask. Use questions and prompts to encourage children to observe and identify feelings and perspectives (see Chapter 5 in this text). Research by Hawkins (2014) found that preschool teachers needed to introduce the literature with guided questions or comments to orient the children to the social justice issues highlighted in the texts. Open-ended and higher-order questioning techniques encouraged deeper reflection and were beneficial for children's development.

- **Cultivate a community of learners**—Ensure that all children see themselves positively reflected in the design and implementation of learning environments, interactions, and materials (NAEYC, 2019a). Create a classroom that fosters respect—where children trust and care for each other. Even when complex issues are addressed, children need to feel emotionally safe. As a class, create classroom guidelines centered on mutual respect. These can include listening when others are speaking and taking turns. Developing a community of learners also means a classroom where everyone learns from and with each other, as the children in Dr. Escamilla's class do. When Zaid and Jason interact with their peers, they learn about similarities, differences, and the importance of respecting one another. Through these interactions, children learn a lot about themselves and others.

- **Involve families in the design and implementation of learning activities**—Build on children's and families' knowledge as community members, sparking interest and engagement (NAEYC, 2019). Recognize that what children learn in their homes and communities is relevant to in-school learning (Wright, 2021). Invite families to share their experiences. Reflect on your assumptions and biases as you interact with children and families (see Chapter 6 of this text).

- **Listen to your students and embrace curiosity**—Isauro and his colleagues learned from their students by listening to their stories. Children naturally want to learn about the world. Do not ignore or discourage your students' questions, even if they make you uncomfortable; instead, follow their lead (Boutte, 2008; Wild, 2023b). When children form conclusions without critical conversations, it can unintentionally reinforce racism and discrimination (Tatum, 2015, 2017; Wright, 2021).

- **Be prepared for difficult conversations**—Grade-level teams and colleagues can serve as resources for brainstorming ways to address difficult situations in the classroom. Activities such as role-playing with colleagues help you practice conversations to prepare for impromptu situations (Kimura et al., 2021).

As you develop your teaching strategies and literacy activities, there are a few teaching practices to support your social justice journey with young children. Books related to social justice issues should be

- included in classroom libraries and be freely accessible to children;
- integrated into the curriculum—as read-alouds, author and illustrator studies, and other developmentally appropriate activities that are meaningful and promote social justice (Bersh, 2013; Leija & Fránquiz, 2021);
- provided as artifacts in culturally relevant dramatic play areas (Salinas-González et al., 2019);
- consulted for topics for small and large group discussions and children's early journal writing (Alvarez, 2018; López-Robertson, 2021); and
- used as references for children's drawing and art-based projects integrated with collections of loose parts (buttons, shells, ribbons) to inspire play (Harper, 2016).

## CLOSING REFLECTIONS

The preschool and kindergarten years are crucial in shaping cultural and racial understandings and forming attitudes toward diversity and difference. As an early childhood educator, you are vital in creating equitable spaces for children. Enhancing your curriculum with social justice topics through picture books helps cultivate a more equitable world and helps develop more empathetic and critical minds. When instruction and curriculum are rooted in children's experiences, they can deepen their understanding of social justice and equity (Boutte, 2008; Souto-Manning, 2013). Picture books offer a way to explore current social issues and ideologies. They significantly influence the development of children's identities, behaviors, and attitudes (Galda & Cullinan, 2006). They are powerful tools for teachers who aim to foster empathy, respect, and acceptance in their students. They are also powerful tools for educators learning to respect and accept their students' cultures, languages, and identities. Engaging children in meaningful conversations about their world is an effective way to learn about others' stories and experiences. By enhancing the curriculum with picture books that teach social justice, teachers lay the foundation for children to become global citizens.

**TRY THIS!**

1. Create indoor and outdoor stations where children can browse books related to social justice issues and themes. Add comfortable seating areas for children to sit, read, and discuss with their peers. Listen to children's conversations to help guide your child-directed curriculum.
2. Organize lending libraries for opportunities to strengthen school–home connections and family participation and engagement. Encourage families to share their stories with you and incorporate them into learning activities. Have children demonstrate their learning through drawings, discussions, and writings.
3. Select theme-related books connected to children's cultural and linguistic heritage to help them develop their bicultural and bilingual identity. Place relevant children's books in learning centers to reflect a topic or theme of children's interest.

## CHAPTER 8

# Picture Books and Authentic Assessment for Social Justice—Educators, Children, and Families as Authors

*Isauro M. Escamilla*

If today's children grow up with literature that is multicultural, diverse, and decolonized, we can begin the work of healing our nation and world through humanizing stories.—Ebony E. Thomas, 2016

### Chapter Objectives

1. Define and examine how children's picture books can be connected to children's language and literacy assessment.
2. Identify the key forms and functions of learning stories.
3. Explore instructional and assessment connections between children's picture books and learning stories.
4. Share examples of learning stories as affirming children's identities and home/community relationships.

This chapter extends elements first introduced throughout the text on the value of teacher inquiry, documentation, and reflection for linking picture books, social justice and equity, and authentic assessment. We specifically focus on using *Learning Stories*, conceptualized and implemented by educators in New Zealand as textual and visual stories to be shared with children and families (Carr & Lee, 2012, 2019). In discussing these benefits, I present two Learning Stories that illustrate key concepts and practices for selecting picture books representing preschool children's life experiences to support bilingualism and validate children's feelings and interests. Each Learning Story example is paired with specific picture books for children to explore vocabulary, language, characters, and illustrations to address children's inquiries about cultural traditions and current social issues. I share examples of how teacher inquiry and documentation can integrate picture books with social justice content as a form of authentic assessment.

### Three Goals for Learning Stories

Learning Stories are visual and written narratives whose purpose is to (1) elevate the image of children as bilingual learners, (2) emphasize observation and documentation as authentic assessment, and (3) affirm all children's cultural, familial, and language identities (Carr & Lee, 2012, 2019).

## RESPONDING TO CHILDREN'S INDIVIDUAL CONCERNS THROUGH PICTURE BOOKS

In the first example, I discuss Julián losing his first baby tooth in the classroom. My teacher colleague, Sahara Gonzalez, and I wrote this Learning Story to showcase this milestone in Julián's life and explain how we used the picture book *The Tooth Fairy Meets El Ratón Pérez* (Colato Laínez, 2010) to help Julián understand this significant moment from a multicultural perspective. The second example is based on a Learning Story written for Zahid that captures family events at home and at the border between Mexico and the United States. In this instance, the teachers incorporated the picture book *A Movie in My Pillow/Una película en mi almohada* (Argueta, 2007) and "Los Zapatos de Papá" [Dad's Shoes], a children's song in Spanish, into the curriculum as a response to concerns and questions that Zahid raised while playing and learning in the classroom.

Both Learning Stories portray the children as competent learners and agentic and valued classroom community members in ways that formal early language and literacy assessments might not fully capture. For example, the use of the visual arts—painting and photography—in the Learning Stories extends children's learning by drawing attention to visuals, languages, characters, and content found in carefully selected picture books.

## STRENGTHENING CHILDREN'S IMAGE AS ENGAGED LEARNERS THROUGH LEARNING STORIES AND PICTURE BOOKS

Effective instruction provides differentiated and individualized support to ensure that all children are seen, heard, and understood. Picture books play a key role in this process by helping children, teachers, and families strengthen how they relate to one another. The teaching team profiled in this chapter worked for several years engaging with children's ideas, dilemmas, and questions to develop authentic assessments using children's picture books and visual and written narratives known as Learning Stories.

## What Are Learning Stories?

Learning Stories are stories or real-life tales written by teachers for children in their classrooms. These stories capture specific "small moments" or events from the children's lives. Teachers document these moments through photographs, videos, children's drawings, dictations, paintings, or artifacts, and teachers' creative writings. As *story composers*—storytellers—they craft Learning Stories based on their knowledge of individual children and the child's specific interests, concerns, or inquiries (Carr & Lee, 2012, 2019; Escamilla et al., 2021). Learning stories have been used in New Zealand with bicultural/bilingual Maori children; they are relatively rarely used in the United States with bilingual children.

The teachers in my former preschool classroom started writing Learning Stories in 2017, but before that, they had developed the skills and dispositions to document and create records of what children accomplished and learned in the classroom and to share these records and documentation with the children and their families. My colleagues and I also used this documentation as sources for collaborative reflection in a site-based inquiry group to generate a deeper understanding of our teaching practices, philosophies, strategies, and goals (for a detailed account of our specific inquiry group experiences, see Escamilla & Meier, 2018).

### Key Components of a Learning Story

A Learning Story has the following components:

1. A title and author's name
2. A few photographs that illustrate the story being told
3. A description of the moment(s) or event(s) that caught the teacher's attention
4. An analysis and interpretation of those moments or events
5. A (tentative) plan to further the child's learning experiences
6. The child's family's perspective on the Learning Story and on their child's learning
7. Connections to assessment measures as (or if) required by the school or school district

## "JULIAN LOSES HIS FIRST BABY TOOTH"—A LEARNING STORY ILLUSTRATING A CHILDHOOD MILESTONE

This three-page Learning Story was originally written in English since it is the preferred language of Julián's family. In "Julián Loses His First Baby Tooth" (see Figure 8.1), the teachers intentionally used certain

**Figure 8.1. Pages from Julián's Learning Story.**

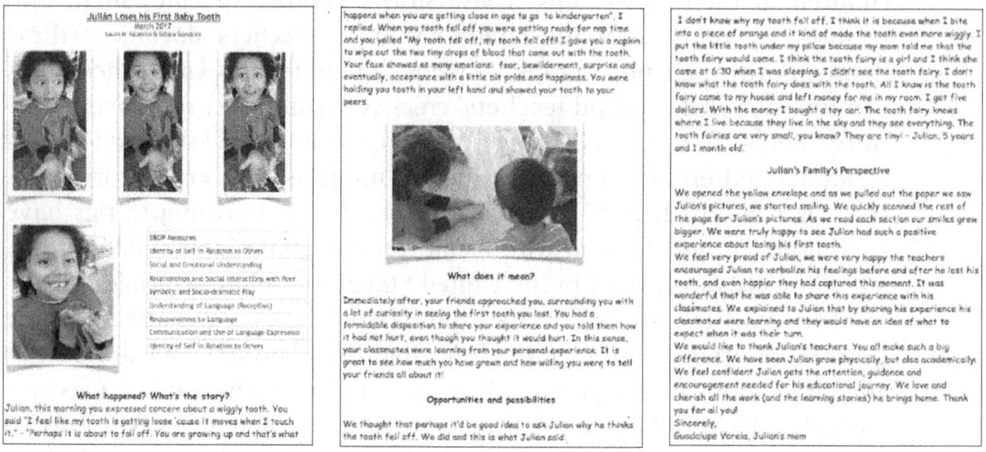

Julián Loses his First Baby Tooth

March 2017

DRDP Measures
Identity of Self in Relation to Others
Social and Emotional Understanding
Relationships and Social Interactions with Peer
Symbolic and Socio-dramatic Play
Understanding of Language (Receptive)
Responsiveness to Language
Communication and Use of Language Expression
Identity of Self in Relation to Others

What happened? What's the story?

Julian, this morning you expressed concern about a wiggly tooth. You said "I feel like my tooth is getting loose 'cause it moves when I touch it." - "Perhaps it is about to fall off. You are growing up and that's what happens when you are getting close in age to go to kindergarten", I replied. When you teeth fell off you were getting ready for nap time and you yelled "My tooth fell off, my tooth fell off!! I gave you a napkin to wipe out the two tiny drops of blood that came out with the tooth. Your face showed so many emotions: fear, bewilderment, surprise and eventually, acceptance with a little bit pride and happiness. You were holding you tooth in your left hand and showed your tooth to your peers.

What does it mean?

Immediately after, your friends approached you, surrounding you with a lot of curiosity in seeing the first tooth you lost. You had a formidable disposition to share your experience and you told them how it had not hurt, even though you thought it would hurt. In this sense, your classmates were learning from your personal experience. It is great to see how much you have grown and how willing you were to tell your friends all about it!

Opportunities and possibilities

We thought that perhaps it'd be good idea to ask Julian why he thinks the tooth fell off. We did and this is what Julian said:

I don't know why my tooth fell off. I think it is because when I bite into a piece of orange and it kind of made the tooth even more wiggly. I put the little tooth under my pillow because my mom told me that the tooth fairy would come. I think the tooth fairy is a girl and I think she came at 6:30 when I was sleeping. I didn't see the tooth fairy. I don't know what the tooth fairy does with the tooth. All I know is the tooth fairy came to my house and left money for me in my room. I got five dollars. With the money I bought a toy car. The tooth fairy knews where I live because they live in the sky and they see everything. The tooth fairies are very small, you know? They are tiny! - Julian, 5 years and 1 month old.

Julian's Family's Perspective

We opened the yellow envelope and as we pulled out the paper we saw Julian's pictures, we started smiling. We quickly scanned the rest of the page for Julian's pictures. As we read each section our smiles grew bigger. We were truly happy to see Julian had such a positive experience about losing his first tooth.
We feel very proud of Julian, we were very happy the teachers encouraged Julian to verbalize his feelings before and after he lost his tooth, and even happier they had captured this moment. It was wonderful that he was able to share this experience with his classmates. We explained to Julian that by sharing his experience his classmates were learning and they would have an idea of what to expect when it was their turn.
We would like to thank Julian's teachers. You all make such a big difference. We have seen Julian grow physically, but also academically. We feel confident Julian gets the attention, guidance and encouragement needed for his educational journey. We love and cherish all the work (and the learning stories) he brings home. Thank you for all you!
Sincerely,
Guadalupe Varela, Julian's mom

words to describe Julián's possible feelings after studying and reflecting on a set of sequential photographs (see Figure 8.2) that show Julián going through a range of emotions upon losing his first baby tooth (an event that positions him as a classroom leader since he is the first child in the classroom to achieve this milestone; see Figure 8.3). In this story, the teacher captured Julián's image as a socially and emotionally competent young learner under the subheading "What Happened? What's the Story?" To complement the Learning Story the teachers suggested including children's books related to Julián's experience of losing a tooth for the first time. One of the books that the teachers selected was *The Tooth Fairy Meets El Ratón Pérez* (Colato Laínez, 2010).

**Figure 8.2. Julián goes through a range of emotions upon losing his last baby tooth.**

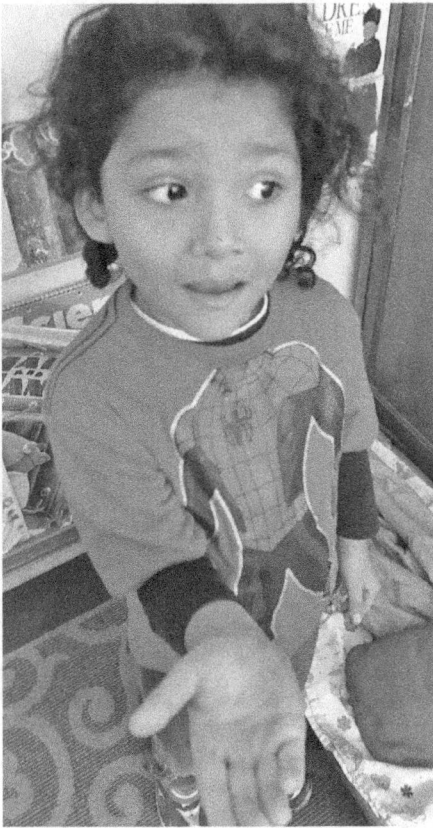

**Figure 8.3. Friends surround Julián to see his tooth.**

The following excerpt is from Julián's Learning Story, written for him when he lost his first baby tooth in the classroom (see Figure 8.4).

### Excerpt from Julian's Learning Story

*Julian, when your tooth fell off you were getting ready for naptime, and you yelled "My tooth fell off, my tooth fell off!" I gave you a napkin to wipe off the two tiny drops of blood that came out with the tooth. Your face showed so many emotions: fear, bewilderment, surprise, and eventually, acceptance with a little bit of pride and happiness.*

In this Learning Story, Julián becomes the main character of his own story, a story that includes photographs that serve as illustrations similar to images found in children's picture books. This Learning Story portrays Julián as a child capable of remarkable self-control, although also conceivably experiencing fear and bewilderment as he was surprised by suddenly losing his first tooth. In the section dedicated to analyzing the story, the teacher wrote:

**Figure 8.4. Julian shows off his baby tooth.**

*What does it mean? Immediately after, your friends approached you, surrounding you with a lot of curiosity in seeing the first tooth you lost. You had a formidable disposition to share your experience, and you told them how it had not hurt, even though you thought it would hurt. In this sense, your classmates were learning from your personal experience. It is great to see how much you have grown and how willing you were to tell your friends all about it!*

Through this Learning Story we see Julián as a classroom leader in an unexpected event, as a child showing a range of emotions in public, and as a volunteer who shared his experience with his peers. Julián, then, becomes a character who acts in his own story.

The family's written response to Julián's Learning Story described him as a courageous little boy facing a potentially intimidating situation, such as losing a front tooth for the first time. Julián's parents acknowledged, over time, that they had seen their son grow physically and academically.

*Response from Julián's parents to his Learning Story: We opened the yellow envelope and as we pulled out the paper and saw Julián's pictures, we started smiling. We quickly scanned the rest of the page for Julián's pictures. As we read each section our smiles grew bigger. We were truly happy to see Julian had such a positive experience about losing his first tooth. We feel very proud of Julián, we were very happy the teach-ers encouraged Julián to verbalize his feelings before and after he lost his tooth, and even happier they had captured this moment. It was wonderful that he was able to share this experience with his classmates. We explained to Julián that by sharing his experience his classmates were learning, and they would have an idea of what to expect when it was their turn. We would like to thank Julián's teachers. You all make such a big difference. We have seen Julian grow physically, but also academically. We feel confident Julian gets the attention, guidance, and encouragement needed for his educa-tional journey. We love and cherish all the work (and learning stories) he brings home. Thank you for all you do.—Guadalupe V., Julián's mom.*

The Learning Story of Julián and his baby tooth highlights a personal event in school that crosses over to his home life. Teachers, children, and families share and celebrate this developmental milestone, which holds significant cultural value for the family. As such, it becomes a treasured ar-tifact shared between home and school. This Learning Story is an authen-tic assessment, portraying Julián as an active, collaborative community member through textual and visual narratives. The teachers kept a copy of Julián's Learning Story in a see-through folder in the classroom, along with other Learning Stories of events of great importance to children. These Learning Stories became picture books for the classroom commu-nity, similar to identity texts with pictures that children could revisit and "read" on their own or with the help of a teacher. To help Julián and all the children become familiar with the experience of losing their first baby tooth, I shared that growing up in Veracruz, Mexico, every time a child lost a tooth, the tradition was that the tooth was thrown over the roof of the house. A little mouse would collect it at night and would leave a coin under the child's pillow while he slept.

In the children's picture book *The Tooth Fairy Meets el Ratón Pérez* by René Colato Laínez a delightful story unfolds when Miguelito, a young Mexican American boy, loses a tooth. A twinkly Tooth Fairy and her Latin American counterpart, el Ratón Pérez (an intrepid, Spanish-speaking small mouse), both appear to claim the tooth. Their encounter turns into a humorous tug-of-war, with each pulling the tooth in opposite direc-tions. "This is Miguelito's house, and I collected his papá's, mamá's, and his abuelitos' teeth," declares the mouse. However, during their squabble, the tooth flies out of their grasp and lands between the books on a nearby shelf. The Tooth Fairy and Ratón Pérez must then join forces to retrieve it. Picture books like this one integrate cultural traditions and allow young children to see their lives and identities reflected within the pages, a genre still characterized by a continued lack of diversity (Short, 2018).

Julián and his preschool peers may not consciously recognize the story of *The Tooth Fairy Meets El Ratón Pérez* as a metaphor for growing up in two cultures, but this culturally responsive story does model how to successfully negotiate a bicultural life by celebrating both aspects of Miguelito's Mexican American heritage. Throughout the story, Colato Laínez features bilingual expressions and exclamations seamlessly embedded in the dialogue and particularly in the conversation between the tooth fairy and Ratón Pérez (see Table 8.1)

Thanks to this conversation, the children in Julián's preschool class subtly learned about two contrasting folktales, one based on European folklore and one with roots in Mexico and Central America. As Thomas (2016) states, "Within the context of schools facing dwindling budgets and constrained choices, it is important that educators' book choices reflect the needs, concerns, and everyday lives of children" (p. 118). The integration of culturally relevant books in the preschool classroom is of critical importance, especially for the increasing number of children living across borders in two cultures and languages, as is the case of Julián, a third-generation child of a family with origins in Mexico, whose parents speak more English than Spanish and whose grandparents speak only Spanish. Colato Laínez's picture book with conversation in English and Spanish is one way to expose children to the language spoken by grandparents.

From Julián's perspective (as described in the Learning Story), this is the story he chooses to live by and which is as valid as Colato Laínez's, his teacher's, or anyone else's traditional tales on what happens when children lose their baby teeth:

**Table 8.1. Vocabulary in Spanish from *The Tooth Fairy Meets el Ratón Pérez* Picture Book**

| Words in Spanish | Words in English |
| --- | --- |
| Mi diente | My tooth |
| Señorita | Young lady |
| Ratón | Mouse |
| Miguelito | Little Miguel |
| Papá | Dad |
| Mamá | Mom |
| Abuelitos | Grandparents |
| ¡Es mio! | It's mine! |
| ¿Dónde está mi diente? | Where is my tooth? |

*I don't know why my tooth fell off. I think it is because when I bite into a piece of orange, and it kind of made the tooth even more wiggly. I put the little tooth under my pillow because my mom told me that the tooth fairy would come. I think the tooth fairy is a girl and I think she came at 6:30 when I was sleeping. I didn't see the tooth fairy. I don't know what the tooth fairy does with the tooth. All I know is the tooth fairy came to my house and left money for me in my room . I got five dollars. With the money I bought a toy car. The tooth fairy knows where I live because they live in the sky and they see everything. The tooth fairy is small, you know? They are tiny!*

After devoting several years to collaborative inquiry and documentation works, my colleagues and I were well-positioned to create Learning Stories such as "Julián Loses His First Baby Tooth" and to link this story with picture books with social justice and equity content. In doing so, we learned to break down Learning Stories into their constituent elements, feature their pedagogical insights, include the voices of the children and their families, and integrate their mandated assessment measures (see Table 8.2). Essentially, the Learning Story became an authentic assessment pathway to showcase children's talents and to reveal them to teachers and families.

## AFFIRMING CHILDREN'S IDENTITIES THROUGH LEARNING STORIES AND CHILDREN'S PICTURE BOOKS

Learning stories also have the potential to showcase children's developing abilities to address political and social issues. Through these stories, children can problem-solve and research possible ways to address these challenges in an agentic manner. Learning Stories can be a meaningful form of authentic assessment, capturing children as problem-solvers who actively seek information, share ideas, present findings to their peers, and utilize maps and other visual tools. These stories highlight how children develop digital literacy skills in two languages while also showcasing their interest in and understanding of social justice and equity challenges, both within the United States and across international borders.

In the Learning Story "Bajo el Mismo Sol" (Under the Same Sun), written in 2017, I discovered the power of Learning Stories to narrate and represent culture and language by reflecting on specific connections to my own transnational U.S./Mexican cultural and linguistic history and identity. I wrote this Learning Story as a response to 5-year-old Zahid's initiative and interest in documenting his father's story and journey, as well as a response to the negative rhetoric that took place in the last months of the 2016 presidential campaign (Zahid is introduced in Chapter 7 of this text). At that time, the Republican presidential candidate Donald Trump

**Table 8.2. Components and Descriptions of a Learning Story**

| Components and Descriptions of a Learning Story | | Example |
|---|---|---|
| Title | Reflects the main message or topic in the story and highlights the child's efforts, accomplishments, or challenge and success. | *Julian Loses His First Baby Tooth!* |
| Photographs | The number of photographs varies depending on what the teacher thinks is best to illustrate the written narrative, highlighting children's actions, participation, engagement, and interactions in their play. | |
| Description of specific moment(s) or event(s) that caught the teacher's attention | The teacher writes directly to children using the first-person singular pronoun "I" to let the child know what they noticed, observed, or witnessed the child doing or saying. | *Julián, when your tooth fell out you were getting ready for naptime, and you yelled in English "My tooth fell off, my tooth fell off!" I gave you a napkin to wipe off the two tiny drops of blood that came out with the tooth. Your face showed so many emotions, fear, bewilderment, surprise . . .* |
| Analysis and interpretation of moments or events | The teacher writes a pedagogical reflection which shares insights on the meaning of memorable moments or events depicted in the story in terms of the child's ongoing learning. | *You had a formidable disposition to share your experience and you told them how it had not hurt, even though you thought it would hurt. In this sense, your classmates were learning from your personal experience.* |
| A (tentative) plan to further the child's learning experiences | Sometimes referred to as *opportunities and possibilities*, this is a plan with potential activities, resources, or materials needed to support children in deeper exploration of their ideas, questions, interests, and concerns. | *We thought it would be a good idea to ask Julian why he thinks the tooth fell out and write down his theory to share with his family.* |
| Family perspective on the Learning Story or child's learning | This is an opportunity for children's families to express how they see their children in their learning journey and what they find valuable in the learning story. | *We opened the yellow envelope and as we pulled out the paper, we saw Julian's pictures and we started smiling. As we read each section our smiles grew bigger. We were truly happy to see Julián had such a positive experience about losing his first baby tooth.* |

*(continued)*

**Table 8.2.** *(continued)*

| Components and Descriptions of a Learning Story | | Example |
|---|---|---|
| Connections to assessment | Depending on each school or district requirements or expectations on producing evidence of children's learning, this is where teachers connect the story content to assessments measures on different learning areas, domains, milestones. | Desired Results Developmental Profile (DRDP) Measures observed:<br>• Identity of Self in Relation to Others<br>• Social and Emotional Understanding<br>• Understanding of Language (Receptive)<br>• Responsiveness to Language<br>• Communication and Use of Language Expression |

publicly expressed his disdain for immigrants of Latin American origin, especially immigrants from Mexico, and specifically Mexican men, whom he called "malos hombres" (bad men) and rapists, and who, he claimed, engaged in drug trafficking, though some, he assumed, were okay. When Mr. Trump's rhetoric hit the mainstream media (and is now repeated during Trump's second term), even the youngest children in our preschool class were aware of his message calling for a higher and stronger wall at the Mexico and United States border.

## ZAHID'S LEARNING STORY OF HIS DAD'S JOURNEY FROM MEXICO TO THE UNITED STATES

This compelling Learning Story, written to and for Zahid, tells the story of a highly creative child who goes to great lengths to understand the physical, political, and figurative barriers that keep his family from being reunited in the United States. Zahid's Learning Story is documented in a series of photographs and video clips that reveal Zahid as a critical thinker aware of the political context in which the events depicted in the story occur. Zahid's Learning Story is four pages long and was initially written in Spanish, which is the language spoken by both Zahid and his family.

One morning, Zahid started telling his classmates a story in Spanish that involved his dad, who was in Mexico trying to cross *la frontera* [the border] to reunite with his family. That day, on more than one occasion, I overheard bits of Zahid's story when he was conversing with his friends. Perhaps I didn't fully capture its significance at that moment, but I took a few observational notes to document and help me remember that moment. I documented Zahid's serious tone, the topic of his conversation, and the matter-of-fact eloquence of his storytelling. "Observational notes are designed to capture and hold one's observations for later analysis. As such, they are effective narrative tools for capturing and recreating essential elements of a teaching and learning story" (Sisk-Hilton & Meier, 2017, p. 50).

A few days later, while singing a song in Spanish, "Los Zapatos de Papá" [Dad's Shoes], from the classroom's scripted Estrellita curriculum, Zahid remarked that he still remembered the funky smell of his dad's shoes when he took them off upon returning home from work. Zahid also expressed how much he wished he could see his dad again.

Zahid's mom shared with his teachers how concerned she was with the turn of events that took place when her husband was taken into custody by the U.S. Immigration and Customs Enforcement (ICE) agency while attempting to cross the U.S.–Mexico border without proper documentation. All these seemingly unconnected happenings gave me the idea to write two interconnected Learning Stories: "Under the Same Sun" and "Waiting for Dad." The idea of writing directly to Zahid within the framework of a Learning Story helped me sort out my own feelings about a toxic political atmosphere and memorialize the significant social and familial events for Zahid, which carried into the classroom and our community of storytellers.

The two Learning Stories written for Zahid document what he was living at that time—and simultaneously give voice to the experience of many immigrants who risk their lives crossing the U.S. border for the dream of a better life on the other side of the wall. Zahid also expressed part of his story visually in an acrylic painting as he painted tall, colorful buildings with a bright sun. He told his teachers that his dad would see that when he arrived in California to reunite with his family.

Zahid's learning story (see Figures 8.5, 8.6) documents how he made strong use of his cultural identity as an immigrant, family member, and bilingual speaker, and his narrative skills as a storyteller to retell a story he had heard at home and was experiencing and living together with his family. Zahid learned to represent symbolically on a map the journey undertaken by his dad and the many different places where he had been taken while detained by immigration officers. Zahid also learned to navigate the internet, searching for images of the Mexico/U.S. border to assist in his story and connect with his father (see Figure 8.7). This Learning Story documents the perspective of a young child trying to make sense of his family situation amid the national backlash against immigrants, who were used as props and targets to advance a disingenuous and racist political agenda. Costello (2016) refers to the resulting divisiveness, incivility, and

**Figure 8.5. Page 1 of 2 of Zahid's Learning Story.**

# BAJO EL MISMO SOL

## Que paso? Cual es la Historia?

De las varias opciones que te propusimos a Zahid para que continuaras su proyecto la que mas te intereso fue la de pintar en un lienzo tu interpretación de la palabra **frontera**

## Que significado tiene este hecho?

Hasta ahora Zahid no habías demostrado mucho interés en pintar , escribir or representar gráficamente tus ideas. Tu modo preferido de expression es comunicarte verbalmente, y lo haces muy bien!

El hecho de que hayas elegido pinceles y pinturas acrílicas revela que todo niño tiene que ser participe activo de las decisiones que se toman en cuanto al aprendizaje individual de cada uno.

## Que posibilidades surgen?

Zahid, podrías compartir tu historia de aprendizaje con tus compañeros de clase y tu familia.

### Representado la palabra *frontera*

Zahid, me da mucho gusto ver la intención tan seria con la que tomaste la idea de representar la palabra **frontera**. Después de tantas sesiones cantando los sonidos iniciales que corresponden a cada letra del alfabeto en Español, me imagine que querrías deletrear la palabra fonema por fonema, pero no fue así. En lugar de esa opción, decidiste algo mas complejo y quisiste usar pinceles y colores acrílicos para (escribir) representar y definir la palabra frontera como tu la percibes basándote en la experiencias que has vivido con tu familia y en especial con tu padre.

*La frontera*

**Figure 8.6. Page 2 of 2 of Zahid's Learning Story.**

Que opina la familia
de Zahid?

Pienso que es bueno que
mi hijo tenga el apoyo de
sus maestros en la
escuela y que pued
expresar lo que siente y
lo que piensa, aunque
algunas veces me
pregunto si es mejor
evitar el tema por
completo. Estos meses
han sido muy difíciles
para todos en la familia,
pero especialmente para
él, porque él es el mayor.
Él dice que extraña a su
papá, aunque no lo he
visto en mucho tiempo. Y
también dice que quiere
regresarse a México
cuando sea más grande
para estar con su padre.
—Mamá

## El Proceso Creativo

Zahid, durante la creación de tu pintura
demostrarte mucha paciencia ya que había que
esperar de un día a otro a que se secara la primera
capa de pintura antes de aplicar la siguiente.

Seleccionaste el color cafe para pintar el muro
porque ese es el color que viste en las fotos que
aparecieron en la pantalla de la computadora
cuando buscamos imágenes de "frontera". De este
lado del muro querías pintar un sol amarillo por que
eso el lo que tu papa vería al llegar a California, así
como edificios altos de colores con muchas
ventanas. Ojalá que tu y tu papá puedan jugar algún
día bajo el mismo sol.

La frontera                                              2

133

fear as the *Trump effect*, citing the harmful rhetoric when Trump spoke of "deporting millions of Latino immigrants, building a wall between the United States and Mexico, banning Muslim immigrants and even killing the families of Islamist terrorists. He has also called Mexican immigrants 'rapists' and drug dealers" (p. 5).

Through our emergent curriculum, we provided Zahid with differentiated and individualized pedagogical support, cultural understanding, social interaction, and new forms of discourse, research, and symbolic representation. Zahid revealed himself as mapmaker, storyteller, and teacher to his peers by documenting his own learning and sharing his story with his classmates. With his teachers' help and peers' support as an audience, Zahid made connections between what he heard on the news, his dad's detention at the border, and the impact of anti-immigrant rhetoric on his family and community. This kind of knowledge and wisdom is impossible to capture in traditional standardized assessments; only a process/product, such as a Learning Story, can capture the explicit and implicit narrative significance of Zahid's and his family's experiences as well as the depth of his conceptual understanding and representation of borders, separation from loved ones, and feelings of loss. The Learning Story framework captured Zahid's small, storied pieces as an artist and learner attempting to reflect the charged political culture at that time. In the initial section of his Learning Story, "What happened? What's the story?" I wrote the following message directly to Zahid:

**Figure 8.7. Zahid pointing on a map to the line between the United States and Mexico.**

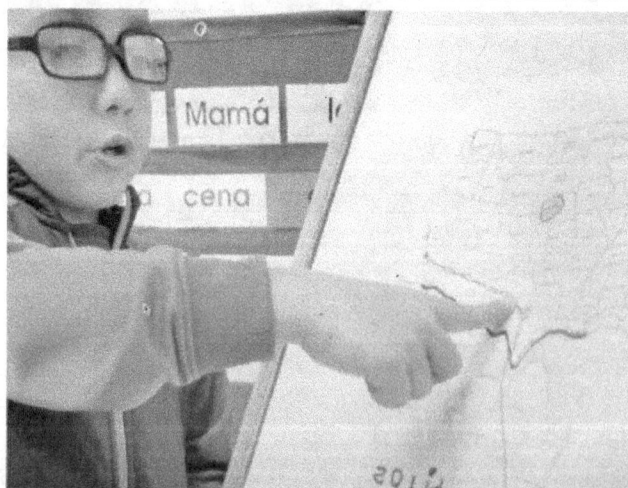

*What happened? What's the story? Zahid, of the several options we proposed to you to continue exploring the topic of the journey of your dad from Mexico to the United States, you chose a canvas, skinny paint brushes, and acrylic colors to represent the word frontera. Until now you had hardly showed interest in using painting tools, the process of writing or making graphic representations of your ideas. Your preferred mode of expression was to communicate orally and you have been doing it quite well! The fact you chose paintbrushes and acrylic paints reveals that every child should have the right to be an active participant when it comes to making decisions about his or her individual learning.*

This Learning Story also helped document and narrate how Zahid's individualized interests became over time the exploration of the concept of family by all the children in the classroom. Zahid's intellectual and artistic work became a focus for the classroom's communal critical pedagogy and exploration of *familia* as a social, cultural, and political construct. While exploring the concept of *familia* with immigrant children, the teachers realized the importance of exposing children to culturally relevant literature. We borrowed books from the public library about stories and tales that resonated with children's and teachers' own *vidas y experiencias* [life and experiences]. At least a dozen children's titles were selected in either Spanish or English, including Spanish-English bilingual books, among them *A Movie in My Pillow/Una película en mi almohada* (Argueta, 2007) written by a local author from El Salvador.

The children enjoyed Argueta's collection of poems in which the main character, a young boy named Jorguito, living in the Mission District of San Francisco—a predominantly Latino community—hasn't forgotten his native El Salvador. The topics of Argueta's poems are the boy's dreams and memories of people, places, and things he left behind, such as *pupusas* (corn tortillas stuffed with cheese, meat, beans, or zucchini), a staple of the Salvadorean cuisine; Neto, Jorguito's best friend; and his mom and grandma. Argueta's memories turned into colorfully illustrated poems helped us see that many of the children in our classroom had "memories" of places from which their parents had emigrated to the United States. Argueta's (2007) poem collection inspired children's and teachers' creativity and imagination. As inquiring teachers (Meier & Henderson, 2007; Meier & Stremmel, 2010; Perry et al., 2012), we often try to find meaning in stories children share. For example, reflecting on the story and completing Zahid's Learning Story, I asked myself, "¿Por qué es importante esta historia?" [What is the significance of this story?]

*¿Por qué es importante esta historia? Representado la palabra frontera —Zahid, me da mucho gusto ver la intención tan seria con la que tomaste la idea de representar la palabra **frontera**. Después de tantas sesiones cantando los sonidos iniciales que corresponden a cada letra del alfabeto en español, me imagine que querrías deletrear la palabra frontera fonema por fonema, pero no fue así. En lugar de esa opción, decidiste algo más complejo y quisiste usar pinceles y colores acrílicos para (escribir) representar y definir la palabra frontera como tú la percibes basándote en las experiencias que has vivido con tu familia y en especial con tu padre.*

[**What is the significance of this story?** Representing the word *frontera*—Zahid, I'm very pleased to see your determination to make a graphic representation of the word *frontera*. After so many sessions singing the initial sounds corresponding to each letter of the alphabet in Spanish, I thought you would be inclined to sound out the word "*frontera*" phoneme by phoneme and spell it out to write it on paper, but that wasn't the case. Instead, you decided to undertake something more complex, and you chose a paint brush and acrylic colors to represent (write) *frontera* the way you perceive it, based on experiences you have lived with your family and especially, with your dad.]

I learned from writing the Learning Stories that meaningful teaching, learning, and assessment for social justice cannot be rushed. It must be nurtured over time and in close collaboration with children, teacher colleagues, and families. Through Learning Stories, we emphasize the value of a narrative-based assessment to document and make visible children's strengths and reimagine children as competent learners and teachers as agentic critical thinkers.

The picture books used as a complement to the Learning Stories in this chapter served as crucial connectors of children's lived experiences and helped Zahid make sense of what he and his family—and perhaps many other (im)migrant families—were experiencing at that time. A book like *A Movie in my Pillow/Una película en mi almohada* (Argueta, 2007) filled a void in young children's literature since children were and still are exposed to so many stories that ignore their perspectives and silence the voices of Latinx (im)migrants (Short, 2018).

## CLOSING REFLECTIONS

The picture books profiled in this chapter all feature stories told from a child's perspective. These culturally relevant picture books capture culturally bound stories from both authors' and children's oral stories.

Reading these stories that relate to their situations helped children understand their own experiences in and out of school. This helped them build a positive sense of self. Teachers working with young children must be open to the unexpected in children's stories in classrooms, homes, and communities. Listening to children's stories allows teachers to learn from children and families, which leads to mutual *respeto* and *confianza*.

Teachers become aware of the importance of picture books in children's learning, carefully selecting and using picture books with engaging storylines and illustrations that speak to children's childhoods (see Appendix A for resources to help you find and select engaging and appropriate books). One of the most challenging tasks in a teacher's day is to assess children learning. Equity-minded teachers often realize that it is almost impossible to capture the essence of a child's learning, knowledge, and wisdom in standardized assessments. As Carr and Lee (2012) remind us, "Formative assessments assess across two main levels: they assess the pieces, while explicitly or implicitly referencing a Big Picture vision. The powerful frameworks in education can also be called the 'big narratives'; in practice, they are made up from small stories" (p. 54). From this perspective, Learning Stories can disrupt the reductive curricular and assessment policies that are endemic in the public schools attended by Latinx children. Additionally, Learning Stories make visible educators' genuine desire to understand children's lived experiences and the cultural and linguistic meanings of those experiences. Furthermore, children's funds of knowledge (Esteban-Guitart & Moll, 2014)—their real-life experiences, inquiries, and interests—can serve as the foundation for joyful learning and authentic assessment that leads to meaningful exploration of diverse cultural traditions and current social issues through children's picture books that playfully connect to children's contemporary childhoods.

## TRY THIS!

- Take observational notes (and audio and video if you can) of a child engaged with a picture book that reveals a new experience, interest, skill, and/or ability.
- Brainstorm ways that your documentation about this child might be turned into a learning story.
- Consider how this small story becomes part of a "big narrative" within a social justice and equity framework.

- In creating your learning story, you can incorporate specific assessment measures from your school or program.
- Share the learning story with the child, the child's family, and/or colleagues, and record some or all of their responses in the learning story as an additional layer of authentic assessment.

# References

Ada, A. F. (2002). *I love Saturdays y domingos* (E. Savadier, Illus.). Atheneum.

Agna, G. (2024). *Finding home: Words from kids seeking sanctuary* (S. Rotner, Illus.). Clarion Books.

Alanís, I., Arreguín, M. G., & Salinas-González, I. (2021). *The essentials: Supporting dual language learners in diverse environments in preschool & kindergarten.* National Association for the Education of Young Children.

Alanís, I., & Iruka, I. U. (Eds.). (2021). *Advancing equity and embracing diversity in early childhood education: Elevating voices and actions.* National Association for the Education of Young Children. https://www.naeyc.org/resources/pubs/books/advancing-equity-embracing-diversity

Alanís, I., & Salinas-González, I. (2023). Integrating families' funds of knowledge into daily teaching practices. In I. Alanis & T. Sturdivant (Eds.), *Focus on developmentally appropriate practice: Equitable and joyful learning in preschool* (pp. 32–36). NAEYC.

Allen, R., Shapland, D. L., Neitzel, J., & Iruka, I. U. (2021). Creating anti-racist early childhood spaces. *Young Children, 76*(2), 49–54.

Alvarez, A. (2018). *Experiential knowledge and project-based learning in bilingual classrooms.* Bank Street Occasional Paper Series, 39. https://doi.org/10.58295/2375-3668.1195

Amberg, A. (2022, January 25). *Grace Lin on diversity and inclusion.* Writers' Rumpus. https://writersrumpus.com/2022/01/25/grace-lin-on-diversity-inclusion/

American Library Association (ALA). (2025). *2024 book ban data.* https://www.ala.org/advocacy/bbooks/book-ban-data

Argueta, J. (2006). *Talking with mother earth/Hablando con madre tierra* (L. Perez, Illus.). Groundwood Books.

Argueta, J. (2007). *A movie in my pillow/Una película en mi almohada* (E. Gómez, illus.). Children's Book Press.

Argueta, J. (2007). *Alfredito flies home/Alfredito regresa volando a su casa* (L. Garay, Illus). Groundwood Books.

Argueta, J. (2009). *Sopa de frijoles/Bean soup* (R. Yockteng, Illus.). Groundwood Books.

Argueta, J. (2013). *Xochitl and the flowers/Xóchitl, la niña de las flores* (C. Angel, Illus.). Lee & Low Books.

Argueta, J. (2016). *Somos como las nubes/We are like the clouds* (A. Ruano, Illus.). Groundwood Books.

Argueta, J. (2017). *Agua, agüita/Water, little water* (F. U. Alcantara, Illus.). Arte Público Press.

Arreguín, M. G., & Alanís, I. (2023). Language of instruction and language of learning in an early childhood dual language classroom: Opening spaces for linguistic freedom and flexibility. In H. L. Smith & K. M. Iyengar (Eds.), *Multicultural language arts for bilingual and dual language classrooms: English-Spanish (pp. 97–115)*. Kendall Hunt.

Arreguín, M. G., Alanís, I., & Salinas-González, I. (2023). An interdisciplinary biliteracy sequence: Aligning daily instruction with the way young bilingual children learn. *Childhood Education, 99*(4), 40–47. https://doi.org/10.1080/00094056.2023.2232280

Arreguín-Anderson, M. G., & Alanís, I. (2019). *Translingual partners in early childhood elementary education: Pedagogies on linguistic and cognitive engagement.* Peter Lang Publishers. https://doi.org/10.3726/b14990

Arreguín-Anderson, M. G., Salinas-González, I., & Alanís, I. (2018). Translingual play that promotes cultural connections. *International Multilingual Research Journal, 12*(4), 273–287.

August, D. L., Carlson, C. D., Barr, C. D., & Bergey, R. (2024). COLLTS: A promising interactive read aloud intervention for three-year-old dual-language learners. *Early Childhood Education Journal, 52*(3), 515–525. https://doi.org/10.1007/s10643-023-01447-1

Baker, C., & Wright, W. E. (2021). *Foundations of bilingual education and bilingualism.* Multilingual Matters.

Baldwin, K. (2018). Preschool through Grade 3: The power of using international picture books with young children. *Young Children, 73*(2), 74–80.

Banker, A. (2020). *I am Brown* (S. Prabhat, Illus.). Lantana Publishing.

Bedford, A.W., & Casbergue, R. (2011). Sharing culturally relevant literature with preschool children in their families. In D. Jones & J. Hagopian (Eds.), *Black Lives Matter at school: An uprising for educational justice* (pp. 59–72). Haymarket Books.

Bersh, L. C. (2013). The curricular value of teaching about immigration through picture book thematic text sets. *Social Studies, 104*(2), 47–56.

Bishop, R. S. (1990). Mirrors, windows, and sliding glass doors. *Perspectives—Gerontological Nursing Association, 6*(3), ix–xi.

Botelho, M. J., & Rudman, M. K. (2009). *Critical multicultural analysis of children's literature: Mirrors, windows, and doors.* Routledge.

Boutte, G. S. (2008). Beyond the illusion of diversity: How early childhood teachers can promote social justice. *The Social Studies, 99*(4), 165–173. https://doi.org/10.3200/TSSS.99.4.165-173

Brittian, A. S., O'Donnell, M., Knight, G. P., Carlo, G., Umana-Taylor, A. J., & Roosa, M. W. (2013). Associations between adolescents' perceived discrimination and prosocial tendencies: The mediating role of Mexican American values. *Journal of Youth and Adolescence 42*, 328–341.

Broderick, J. T., & Hong, S. B. (2011). Introducing the cycle of inquiry system: A reflective inquiry practice for early childhood teacher development. *Early Childhood Research & Practice, 13*(2). http://files.eric.ed.gov.tc.idm.oclc.org/fulltext/EJ956375.pdf

Brooks, W., & McNair, J. C. (2009). "But this story of mine is not unique": A review of research on African American children's literature. *Review of Educational Research, 79*(1), 125–162.

Bruno, E. P., & Iruka, I. U. (2022). Reexamining the Carolina Abecedarian project using an antiracist perspective: Implications for early care and education research. *Early Childhood Research Quarterly, 58*, 165–176.

Cabell, S. Q., Zucker, T. A., DeCoster, J., Melo, C., Forston, L., & Hamre, B. (2019). Prekindergarten interactive book reading quality and children's language and literacy development: Classroom organization as a moderator. *Early Education and Development, 30*(1), 1–18. https://doi.org/10.1080/10409289.2018.1514845

Cambridge University Press. (n.d.). Justice. In *Cambridge Dictionary*. Retrieved September 25, 2025 from https://dictionary.cambridge.org/us/dictionary/english/justice

Cantu, C. V. (2023). Critical content analysis of language in literacy: Identifying discourse and translanguaging in *Esperanza Rising. Journal of Latinos and Education, 22*(5), 2138–2150.

Capshaw, K. & Duane, A. M. (Eds.). (2017). *Who writes for Black children?: African American children's literature before 1900.* University of Minnesota Press.

Cardona Berrio, L., & Arreguín, M. G. (2023). Dichos y adivinanzas: Herramientas culturales que impulsan el éxito académico y el desarrollo cognitivo en el aula bilingüe. *Journal of Bilingual Education Research and Instruction*, Special Issue 2023, 45–58.

Carson, L. R. (2009). "I am because we are:" Collectivism as a foundational characteristic of African American college student identity and academic achievement. *Social Psychology of Education: An International Journal, 12*(3), 327–344. https://doi.org/10.1007/s11218-009-9090-6

Carr, M., & Lee, W. (2019). Learning stories: Pedagogic practices and provocations. In J. Formosinho & J. Peeters (Eds.), *Understanding pedagogic documentation in early childhood education* (pp. 4–31). Routledge.

Carr, M., & Lee, W. (2012). *Learning stories: Constructing learner identities in early education.* SAGE Publications.

Chavous, T. M., Rivas-Drake, D., Smalls, C., Griffin, T., & Cogburn, C. (2008). Gender matters, too: The influences of school racial discrimination and racial identity on academic engagement outcomes among African American adolescents. *Developmental Psychology, 44*(3), 637–654.

Childs, K. R. (2024). *I am more than my name* (B. James, Illus.). EdWhys Publishing.

Christ, T., & Cho, H. (2023). Emergent bilingual students' small group read-aloud discussions. *Literacy Research and Instruction, 62*(3), 203–232. https://doi.org/10.1080/19388071.2022.2085637

Chumdari, S. A., & Budiyono, N. S. (2018). Implementation of thematic instructional model in elementary school. *International Journal of Educational Research 3*, 23–31.

Clark, A. (2020). Cultural relevance and linguistic flexibility in literature discussions with emergent bilingual children. *Bilingual Research Journal, 43*(1), 50–70. https://doi.org/10.1080/15235882.2020.1722974

Clarke, L. W. (2020). Walk a day in my shoes: Cultivating cross-cultural understanding through digital literacy. *The Reading Teacher, 73*(5), 662–665. https://doi.org/10.1002/trtr.1890

Colato Laínez, R. (2010). *The tooth fairy meets El Ratón Pérez* (T. Lintern, Illus.). Tricycle Press.

Colato Laínez, R. (2009). *René has two last names/René tiene dos apellidos.* (F. Graulle-ra Ramírez, Illus.). Arte Público Press.

Colato Laínez, R. (2015). *Waiting for papá/Esperando a papá.* (A. Accardo, Illus.). Piñata Books. Arte Público Press.

Colato Laínez, R. (2016). *Mamá the Alien/Mamá la extraterrestre.* (L. Lacámara, Il-lus.). Children's Books Press.

Cole, J. B., & LaTeef, N. (2021). *African proverbs for all ages* (N. LaTeef, Illus.). Roar-ing Book Press.

Costello, M. B. (2016). *The Trump effect: The impact of the presidential campaign on our nation's schools* [Report]. Southern Poverty Law Center. https://www.splcenter.org/sites/default/files/splc_the_trump_effect.pdf

Culham, R. (2016). *The writing thief: Using mentor texts to teach the craft of writing.* Stenhouse Publishers.

Dahlberg, G., & Moss, P. (2005). *Ethics and politics in early childhood education.* Rout-ledge Falmer.

De Houwer, A. (2009). *Bilingual first language acquisition.* Multilingual Matters.

De Houwer, A. (2021). *Bilingual development in childhood.* Cambridge University Press.

de la Peña, M. (2018). *Carmela full of wishes* (C. Robinson, Illus.). G.P. Putnam's Sons.

DeJulio, S., Martinez, M., Harmon, J., Wilburn, M., & Stavinoha, M. (2022). Read aloud across grade levels: A closer look. *Literacy Practice and Research, 47*(2), 6.

Dennis, E. (2022). *The boy from Mexico: An immigration story of bravery and determina-tion.* Dragonfruit.

Derman-Sparks, L., & Edwards, J. O. (2010). *Anti-bias education for young children and ourselves.* National Association for the Education of Young Children.

Derman-Sparks, L., & Edwards, J. O. (2019). Understanding anti-bias education. *Young Children, 74*(5), 6–13.

Derman-Sparks, L., & Edwards, J. O., with Goins, C. (2020). *Anti-bias education for young children and ourselves* (2nd ed.). National Association for the Education of Young Children.

Derman-Sparks, L., & Ramsey, P. G. (2011). *What if all the kids are white?: Anti-bias multicultural education with young children and families.* Teachers College Press.

Devenny, J. (2021). *Race cars: A children's book about white privilege.* Frances Lincoln Children's Books.

Dyson, A. H. (2003). *The brothers and sisters learn to write: Popular literacies in child-hood and school culture.* Teachers College Press.

Easton, E. (2018). *Enough! 20+ protesters who changed America* (Z. Chen, Illus.). Pen-guin Random House.

Edyburn, K. L., Quirk, M., & Oliva-Olson, C. (2019). Supporting Spanish–English bilingual language development among Latinx dual language learners in ear-ly learning settings. *Contemporary School Psychology, 23*(1), 87–100.

Enriquez, G., Clark, S. R., & Della Calce, J. (2017). Using children's literature for dy-namic learning frames and growth mindsets. *The Reading Teacher, 70*(6), 711–719.

Escamilla, I. M. (2021). Learning stories: Observation, reflection, and narrative in early childhood education. *Young Children, 76*(2), 33–39.

Escamilla, I. M., Alanís, I., & Meier, D. R. (2023). Translanguaging in preschool: Supporting language rights and social justice for Latino/a children, families, and educators. *Contemporary Issues in Early Childhood, 25*(2), 162–185. https://doi.org/10.1177/14639491231164129

Escamilla, I. M., & Meier, D. (2018). The promise of teacher inquiry and reflection: Early childhood teachers as change agents. *Studying Teacher Education, 14*(1), 3–21.

Escayg, K. A. (2024). Starting with the self: Conceptualizing an anti-racist early childhood pedagogy by critiquing white educators' social-emotional competencies. *Contemporary Issues in Early Childhood*, 14639491241273926. https://doi.org/10.1177/14639491241273926

Esteban-Guitart, M. (2021). Advancing the funds of identity theory: A critical and unfinished dialogue. *Mind, Culture, and Activity, 28*(2), 169–179.

Esteban-Guitart, M., & Moll, L. C. (2014). Funds of identity: A new concept based on the funds of knowledge approach. *Culture & Psychology, 20*(1), 31–48.

Evans, S.W. (2012). *We march*. Roaring Press.

Farrell, K. (2020). *V is for voting* (C. Kuhwald, Illus.). Henry Holt.

Fontanella-Nothom, O. (2019). "Why do we have different skins anyway?": Exploring race in literature with preschool children. *Multicultural Perspectives, 21*(1), 11–18. https://doi.org/10.1080/15210960.2019.1572485

Freire, P. (1970). Cultural action and conscientization. *Harvard Educational Review, 40*(3), 452–477.

Galda, L., & Cullinan, B. E. (2006). *Literature and the child*. Thomson Wadsworth.

Gallo, S., & Link, H. (2016). Exploring the borderlands: Elementary school teachers' navigation of immigration practices in a new Latino diaspora community. *Journal of Latinos and Education, 15*(3), 180–196.

García, O. (2009). *Bilingual education in the 21st century: A global perspective*. Wiley-Blackwell.

García, O. (2020). Translanguaging and Latinx bilingual readers. *The Reading Teacher, 73*(5), 557–562.

García, O., & Kleifgen, J. A. (2018). *Educating emergent bilinguals: Policies, programs, and practices for English learners*. Teachers College Press.

García, O., & Wei, L. (2014). *Translanguaging: Language, bilingualism and education*. Palgrave Macmillan.

Gay, G. (2018). *Culturally responsive teaching: Theory, research, and practice*. Teachers College Press.

Genesee, F., Lindholm-Leary, K., Saunders, W., & Christian, D. (2004). *Educating English language learners: A synthesis of research evidence*. Cambridge University Press.

Gerber, M., & Johnson, A. (2008). *Your self-confident baby: How to encourage your child's natural abilities from the very start*. Trade Paper Press.

Gordon, M. (2009). *Roots of empathy: Changing the world child by child*. The Experiment.

Gort, M., & Sembiante, S. F. (2015). Navigating hybridized language learning spaces through translanguaging pedagogy: Dual language preschool teachers' languaging practices in support of emergent bilingual children's performance of academic discourse. *International Multilingual Research Journal, 9*(1), 7–25. https://doi.org/10.1080/19313152.2014.981775

Gutiérrez, K. D. (2008). Developing a sociocritical literacy in the third space. *Reading Research Quarterly, 43*(2), 148–164. https://doi.org/10.1598/RRQ.43.2.3

Harper, L. J. (2016). Using picture books to promote social-emotional literacy. *Young Children, 71*(3), 80–86.

Harper, L. J., & Trostle-Brand, S. (2010). More alike than different: Promoting respect through multicultural books and literacy strategies. *Childhood Education 86*(4), 224–233.

Harry, B., & Ocasio-Stoutenberg, L. (2020). *Meeting families where they are: Building equity through advocacy with diverse communities.* Teachers College Press.

Harste, J. C. (2000). Supporting critical conversations in classrooms. In K. M. Pierce (Ed.)., *Adventuring with books: A booklist for pre-K–grade 6* (12th ed.) (pp. 507–554). National Council of Teachers of English.

Hawkins, K. (2014). Teaching for social justice, social responsibility and social inclusion: A respectful pedagogy for twenty-first century early childhood education. *European Early Childhood Education Research Journal, 22*(5), 723–738. https://doi.org/10.1080/1350293X.2014.969085

Hayes, C., & Francis, G. (2024). Making waves: Early childhood teachers' experiences with multicultural picture books to promote equitable classrooms. *Early Childhood Education Journal, 52*(7), 1511–1523. https://doi.org/10.1007/s10643-023-01557-w

Helbig, S., & Piazza, S. V. (2020). Let's read a story!: Collaborative meaning making, student engagement, and vocabulary building through the use of interactive read alouds. *Michigan Reading Journal, 53*(1), 15–24. https://scholarworks.gvsu.edu/mrj/vol53/iss1/6/

Helgeland, B. (Director). (2013). *42* [Film]. Warner Brothers.

Helm, J. H., & Katz, L. G. (2010). *Young investigators: The project approach in the early years* (2nd ed.). Teachers College Press.

Helmberger, J. (2020). Representing cultural identity in children's literature: Black children in their communities. In D. Jones & J. Hagopian (Eds.), *Black lives matter at school: An uprising for educational justice* (pp. 33–44). Haymarket Books.

Hisrich, K. E., & McCaffrey, M. (2021). Planning and preparing for read-alouds. *Illinois Reading Council Journal, 49*(2), 12–20. https://doi.org/10.33600/IRCJ.49.2.2021.12

Ho, J. (2023). *Say my name* (K. Le, Illus.). HarperCollins.

Husband, T. (2012). "I don't see color": Challenging assumptions about discussing race with young children. *Early Childhood Education Journal, 39*(6), 365–371.

Husband, T. (2019). Using multicultural picture books to promote racial justice in urban early childhood literacy classrooms. *Urban Education, 54*(8), 1058–1084.

Iftikar, J. S., & Museus, S. D. (2018). On the utility of Asian critical (AsianCrit) theory in the field of education. *International Journal of Qualitative Studies in Education, 31*(10), 935–949. https://doi.org/10.1080/09518398.2018.1522008

Iruka, I. U., Curenton, S. M., Durden, T. R., & Escayg, K. A. (2020). *Don't look away: Embracing anti-bias classrooms.* Gryphon House.

Iruka, I. U., Durden, T. R., Escayg, K. A., & Curenton, S. M. (2023). *We are the change we seek: Advancing racial justice in early care and education.* Teachers College Press.

Iruka, I. U., Gardner-Neblett, N., Telfer, N. A., Ibekwe-Okafor, N., Curenton, S. M., Sims, J., Sansbury, A. B., & Neblett, E. W. (2022). Effects of racism on child development: Advancing antiracist developmental science. *Annual Review of Developmental Psychology, 4*(1), 109–132.

Irwin, V., Zhang, J., Wang, K., Jung, J., Kessler, E., Tezil, T., Alhassani, S., Filby, A., AIR, Dilig, R., & Bullock Mann, F. (2024). *Report on the Condition of Education 2024* (NCES 2024–144). National Center for Education Statistics. https://nces.ed.gov /use-work/resource-library/report/compendium/condition-education-2024

Iyengar, M. M. (2009), *Tan to tamarind: Poems about the color brown* (J. Akib, Illus.). Children's Books Press.

Johnson, A., Barker, E., & Cespedes, M. V. (2024). Reframing research and assessment practices: Advancing an antiracist and anti-ableist research agenda. *Educational measurement: Issues and practice, 43*(4), 95–105.

Johnson, W. F., Vlach, S. K., & Leija, M. G. (2025). Enacting reading comprehension: Using diverse literature to engage children's critical, sociopolitical knowledge. *Reading Research Quarterly, 60*(1). https://doi.org/10.1002/rrq.584

Jones, D. (2020). Centering the youngest Black children: An interview with Takiema Bunche-Smith. In D. Jones & J. Hagopian (Eds.), *Black Lives Matter at school: An uprising for educational justice* (pp. 150–157). Haymarket Books.

Jones, D., & Hagopian, J. (Eds.) (2020). *Black Lives Matter at school: An uprising for educational justice*. Haymarket Books.

Jones, E., & Stacey, S. (2018). *Emergent curriculum in early childhood settings: From theory to practice*. Redleaf Press.

Keats, E. J. (1962). *The snowy day*. Viking Books.

Kelly, L. B. (2022). A translanguaging read-aloud. *The Reading Teacher 75*(6), 763–766. https://doi.org/10.1002/trtr.2086

Kendi, I. X. (2019). *How to be an antiracist*. One World.

Kesler, T., Mills, M., & Reilly, M. (2020). I hear you: Teaching social justice in interactive read-aloud. *Language Arts, 97*(4), 207–222. https://doi.org/10.58680/ la202030511

Kim, S. J., & Heyneman, S. P. (2015). Korean-origin kindergarten children's response to African-American characters in race-themed picture books. *Education Research International, 2015*(1), 986342.

Kimura, A. M., Antón-Oldenburg, M., & Pinderhughes, E. E. (2021). Developing and teaching an anti-bias curriculum in a public elementary school: Leadership, K–1 teachers', and young children's experiences. *Journal of Research in Childhood Education, 36*(2), 183–202. https://doi.org/10.1080/02568543.2021.1912222

Kohlberg, L. (1971). *Stages of moral development as a basis for moral education*. Center for Moral Education, Harvard University. https://www.degruyterbrill.com /document/doi/10.3138/9781442656758-004/html

Kosara, R., & Mackinlay, J. (2013). Storytelling: the next step for visualization. *Computer, 46*(5), 44–50. https://doi.org/10.1109/MC.2013.36

Kress, G. (2010). *Multimodality: A social semiotic approach to contemporary communication*. Routledge.

Kuh, L. P., LeeKeenan, D., Given, H., & Beneke, M. R. (2016). Moving beyond anti-bias activities: Supporting the development of anti-bias practices. *Young*

*Children, 71*(1), 58–65. https://www.naeyc.org/resources/pubs/yc/mar2016/moving-beyond-anti-bias-activities

Kuh, L., LeeKeenan, D., & Jaboneta, N. (2024). Teaching for equity and agency. *Young Children, 79*(3), 52–61. https://www.antibiasleadersece.com/wp-content/uploads/2024/09/Teaching-for-Equity-and-Agency_-Intenti.at-Support-Anti-Bias-Education-_-NAEYC.pdf

Ladson-Billings, G. (1995). But that's just good teaching! The case for culturally relevant pedagogy. *Theory Into Practice, 34*(3), 159–165. https://doi.org/10.1080/00405849509543675

Lara, G., & Leija, M. G. (2014). Discussing gender roles and equality by reading "Max: The Stubborn Little Wolf." *Social Studies and the Young Learner, 27*(2), 22–25.

Larrick, N. (1965). The all-white world of children's books. *Saturday Review, 48*, 63–65.

Leander, K., & Boldt, G. (2013). Rereading "A pedagogy of multiliteracies": Bodies, texts, and emergence. *Journal of Literacy Research, 45*(1), 22–46.

Lee, S., Adair, J. K., Payne, K. A., & Barry, D. (2022). Revisioning fairness as social justice in early childhood education. *Early Childhood Education Journal, 50* (1083–1095).

Leija, M. G., & Fránquiz, M. E. (2021). Building bridges between school and home: Teacher, parents, and students examining Latinx immigrant experiences. In G. Onchwari & S. Keengwe (Eds.), *Bridging family-teacher relationships for ELL and immigrant students* (pp. 100–121). IGI Global. https://doi.org/10.4018/978-1-7998-4712-0

Leija, M. G., Martinez, M., & DeJulio, S. (2023). Beyond leveled readers: Finding engaging books to support beginning readers. *Texas Journal of Literacy Education, 10*(1), 8.

Leija, M. G., & Ramírez, R. (2023). Culturally sustaining interdisciplinary biography project: Pedagogical practices of a third-grade teacher. *Journal of Bilingual Education Research and Instruction*, Special Issue 2023, 3–19. https://tabe.org/images/Documents/jberi-special-issue-2023-final-pdf.pdf

Lewison, M., Flint, A. S., & Van Sluys, K. (2002). Taking on critical literacy: The journey of newcomers and novices. *Language Arts, 79*(5), 382–392.

López-Robertson, J. (2021). *Celebrating our cuentos: Choosing and using Latinx literature in elementary classrooms.* Scholastic.

Lynn, M., & Parker, L. (2006). Critical race studies in education: Examining a decade of research on US schools. *Urban Review: Issues and Ideas in Public Education, 38*(4), 257–290.

Lyons, K. S. (2019a). *Going down home with daddy* (D. Minter, Illus.). Peachtree Publishing.

Lyons, K. S. (2019b). *Sing a song: How "Lift Every Voice and Sing" inspired generations* (K. Mallet, Illus.). Nancy Paulsen Books.

Lysaker, J., & Sedberry, T. (2015). Reading difference: Picture book retellings as contexts for exploring personal meanings of race and culture. *Literacy, 49*(2), 105–111.

MacNaughton, G., & Williams, G. (2008). *Techniques for teaching young children: Choices for theory and practice.* Pearson Education Australia.

MacNevin, M., & Berman, R. (2017). The Black baby doll doesn't fit the disconnect between early childhood diversity policy, early childhood educator practice, and children's play. *Early Child Development and Care, 187*(5–6), 827–839.

Madison, M., & Ralli, J. (2021). *Our skin: A first conversation about race.* (I. Roxas, Illus.). Rise.

Madison, M., & Ralli, J. (2024). *We care* (S. Miller, Illus.). Rise.

Manushkin, F. (2018). *Happy in our skin* (L. Tobia, Illus.). Candlewick Press.

McClure, E. L., & Fullerton, S. K. (2017). Instructional interactions: Supporting students' reading development through interactive read-alouds of informational texts. *The Reading Teacher, 71*(1), 51–59. https://doi.org/10.1002/trtr.1576

McGee, L., & Schickedanz, J. (2017). *Repeated interactive read alouds in preschool and kindergarten.* Reading Rockets. https://www.readingrockets.org/topics/comprehension/articles/repeated-interactive-read-alouds-preschool-and-kindergarten

Medina, J. (1999). *My name is Jorge on both sides of the river: Poems in English and Spanish* (F. Vanden Broeck, Illus.). Wordsong/Boyds Mills Press.

Medina, M. (2015). *Mango, Abuela, and me* (A. Dominguez, Illus.). Children's Books Press.

Meier, D., & Henderson, B. (2007). *Learning from young children in the classroom: The art & science of teacher research.* Teachers College Press.

Meier, D., & Stremmel, A. (2010). Reflection through narrative: The power of narrative inquiry in early childhood teacher education. *Journal of Early Childhood Teacher Education, 31*(3), 249–257.

Meltzer, B. (2015). *I am Jackie Robinson* (C. Eliopoulos, Illus.). Rocky Pond Books.

Méndez, Y. S. (2019). *¿De dónde eres?* (J. Kim, Illus.). HarperCollins.

Milner, H. R., IV. (2021). *Start where you are, but don't stay there: Understanding diversity, opportunity gaps, and teaching in today's classrooms.* Harvard Education Press

Milner, H. R., IV Howard, J., Cornelious, T., Best, B. O., & Fittz, L. (2021). Opportunity centered teaching for racial justice in elementary English language arts classrooms. *Language Arts, 99*(1), 48–55.

Moll, L. C., Amanti, C., Neff, D., & Gonzalez, N. (1992). Funds of knowledge for teaching: Using a qualitative approach to connect homes and classrooms. *Theory into Practice, 31*(2), 132–141.

Moll, L. C., & González, N. (1994). Lessons from research with language-minority children. *Journal of Reading Behavior, 26*(4), 439–456. https://doi.org/10.1080/10862969409547862

Morales, A. (2021). *Areli is a dreamer* (L. Uribe, Illus.). Random House Studio.

Morales, Y. (2015). *Niño wrestles the world.* Roaring Brook Press.

Morales, Y. (2018). *Dreamers/Soñadores.* Neal Porter Books.

Morales, Y. (2022, September 14). A journey of transformation: The Zena Sutherland lecture. *The Horn Book.* https://www.hbook.com/story/a-journey-of-transformation-the-zena-sutherland-lecture

Morgan, M. (2016). 'The world is yours': The globalization of hip-hop language. *Social Identities, 22*(2), 133–149.

Muhammad, G. (2020). *Cultivating genius: An equity framework for culturally and historically responsive literacy.* Scholastic Incorporated.

Myers, C. (2013). Young dreamers. *The Horn Book, 89*(6), 10–14.

Naidoo, J. C., & Crandall, H. (2011). Latino children's literature and literacy in school library media centers. *Celebrating cuentos: Promoting Latino children's literature and literacy in classrooms and libraries,* 113–143.

Naqvi, R., McKeogh, A., Thorne, K., and Pfitscher, C. (2013). Dual-language books as an emergent literacy resource: Culturally and linguistically responsive teaching and learning. *Journal of Early Childhood Literacy, 13*(4), 501–528.

National Academies of Sciences, Engineering, and Medicine. (2019). *Vibrant and healthy kids: Aligning science, practice, and policy to advance health equity.* The National Academies Press. https://doi.org/10.17226/25466

National Association for the Education of Young Children. (2019a). *Advancing equity in early childhood education* [Position statement]. https://www.naeyc.org/resources/position-statements/equity

National Association for the Education of Young Children. (2019b). *Professional standards and competencies for early childhood educators.* https://www.naeyc.org/sites/default/files/globally-shared/downloads/PDFs/resources/position-statements/standards_and_competencies_ps.pdf

National Association for the Education of Young Children. (2020). *Developmentally appropriate practice* [Position statement]. https://www.naeyc.org/resources/position-statements/dap/contents

National Association for the Education of Young Children. (2022). *Developmentally appropriate practice in early childhood programs serving children from birth through age 8* (4th ed.).

New London Group. (1996). A pedagogy of multiliteracies: Designing social futures. *Harvard Educational Review, 66*(1), 60–92.

Nguyen, A. (2022). "Children have the fairest things to say": Young children's engagement with anti-bias picture books. *Early Childhood Education Journal, 50*(5), 743–759. https://doi.org/10.1007/s10643-021-01186-1

O'Byrne, W. I., Houser, K., Stone, R., & White, M. (2018). Digital storytelling in early childhood: Student illustrations shaping social interactions. *Frontiers in Psychology, 9.* https://doi.org/10.3389/fpsyg.2018.01800

Odeh, M. (2024). *A map for Falasteen* (A. Betawi, Illus.). Henry Holt.

Osorio, S. L. (2018). Toward a humanizing pedagogy: Using Latinx children's literature with early childhood students. *Bilingual Research Journal, 41*(1), 5–22.

Osorio, S. L. (2020). Building culturally and linguistically sustaining spaces for emergent bilinguals: Using read-alouds to promote translanguaging. *The Reading Teacher, 74*(2), 127–135. https://doi.org/10.1002/trtr.1919

Otto, B. (2018). *Language development in early childhood education.* Pearson.

Paris, D. (2012). Culturally sustaining pedagogy: A needed change in stance, terminology, and practice. *Educational Researcher, 41*(3), 93–97. https://doi.org/10.3102/0013189X12441244

Paris, D. (2021). Culturally sustaining pedagogies and our futures. *The Educational Forum, 85*(4), 364–376. https://doi.org/10.1080/00131725.2021.1957634

Paris, D., & Alim, H. S. (Eds.). (2017). *Culturally sustaining pedagogies: Teaching and learning for justice in a changing world.* Teachers College Press.

Paul, M. (2020). *Speak up* (E. Glenn, Illus.). Clarion Books.

Perry, G., Henderson, B., & Meier, D. R. (Eds.) (2012). *Our inquiry, our practice: Undertaking, supporting, and learning from early childhood teacher research(ers).* National Association for the Education of Young Children.

Perry, K. H. (2012). What is literacy?—A critical overview of sociocultural perspectives. *Journal of Language & Literacy Education, 8*(1), 50–71.

Perry, L. (2016). *Skin like mine* (B. Jackson, Illus.). G Publishing.

Pimentel, A. B. (2020). *All the way to the top: How one girl's fight for Americans with
disabilities changed everything* (N. H. Ali, Illus.). Sourcebooks.

Place, S., & Hoff, E. (2016). Effects and noneffects of input in bilingual environments on dual language skills in 2½-year-olds. *Bilingualism: Language and Cog-
nition, 19*(5), 1023–1041. https://doi.org/10.1017/S1366728915000322

Pushkin, I., & Veness, T. (2017). The development of racial awareness and prejudice
in children. In P. Watson (Ed.), *Psychology and race* (pp. 23–42). Routledge.

Quinn, P. C., Lee, K., Pascalis, O., & Tanaka, J. W. (2016). Narrowing in categorical
responding to other-race face classes by infants. *Developmental Science, 19*(3),
362–371. https://doi.org/10.1111/desc.12301

Ramírez-Esparza, N., García-Sierra, A., & Kuhl, P. K. (2016). The impact of early
social interactions on later language development in Spanish-English bilingual infants. *Child Development, 88*(4), 1216–1234.

Ramsey, P. G. (2004). *Teaching and learning in a diverse world: Multicultural education
for young children*. Teachers College Press.

Rinaldi, C. (2006). *In dialogue with Reggio Emilia: Listening, researching and learning*.
Routledge Falmer.

Robin, B. R. (2008). Digital storytelling: a powerful technology tool for the
21st century classroom. *Theory and Practice, 47*(3), 220–228. https://doi.org/10
.1080/00405840802153916

Robinson, C. (2019a). *another*. Atheneum Books.

Robinson, C. (2019b). *Meet-the-Illustrator recording with Christian Robinson*. Teaching
Books. https://school.teachingbooks.net/book_reading.cgi?a=1&id=16457

Rochat, P. (2024). Developmental roots of human self-consciousness. *Journal of Cognitive Neuroscience, 36*(8), 1610–1619.

Rogoff, B. (2003). *The cultural nature of human development*. Oxford University
Press.

Roots of Empathy (2023, Jul 10). *Parenting expert, Mary Gordon, on the importance of
empathy for our future* [Video]. Youtube. https://www.youtube.com/watch?v
=ia9uYIv5fVA

Rose, T. (2019). *M is for melanin*. Little Bee Books.

Rowe, M. L. (2019). Emergent bilingual students' translation practices during
eBook composing. *Bilingual Research Journal, 42*(3), 324–342. https://doi.org
/10.1080/15235882.2019.1632756

Rowe, M. L., & Miller, E. (2016). Multimodal support in early literacy learning:
The role of visual and textual literacy. *Early Childhood Research Quarterly, 35*,
177–187.

Salinas-González, I., Arreguín-Anderson, M. G., & Alanís, I. (2019). Supporting
language through culturally rich dramatic play. *In M. L. Masterson & H. Bohart
(Eds.), Serious fun: Guiding play to extend children's learning* (pp. 35–44). NAEYC.

Sánchez, P., & Landa, M. (2016). Cruzando fronteras: Negotiating the stories of
Latina/o immigrant and transnational children. *Multicultural literature for Latino bilingual children: Their words, their worlds*, 69–82.

Sayer, P. (2013). Translanguaging, Tex-Mex, and bilingual pedagogy: Emergent bilinguals learning through the vernacular. *"TESOL" Quarterly, 47*(1), 63–88.

Seltzer, K. (2020). "My English is its own rule": Voicing a translingual sensibility through poetry. *Journal of Language, Identity and Education, 19*(5), 297–311.

Shimek, C. (2024). "Reading is social": Dialogic responses to interactive read-alouds with nonfiction picture books. *Early Childhood Education Journal, 52*(7), 1615–1624. https://doi.org/10.1007/s10643-023-01590-9

Short, K. G. (2018). What's trending in children's literature and why it matters. *Language Arts, 95*(5), 287–298.

Singleton, G., & Linton, C. (2006). *Courageous conversations about race: A field guide for achieving equity in schools.* Corwin Press.

Sipe, L. R. (2002). Talking back and taking over: Young children's expressive engagement during storybook read-alouds. *The Reading Teacher, 55*(5), 476–483.

Siraj-Blatchford, I., & Sylva, K. (2004). Researching pedagogy in English preschools. *British Educational Research Journal 30*(5), 713–730. https://doi.org/10.1080/0141192042000234665

Sisk-Hilton, S., & Meier, D. R. (2017). *Narrative inquiry in early childhood and elementary school: Learning to teach, teaching well.* Taylor & Francis.

Solórzano, D. G. (1997). Images and words that wound: Critical race theory, racial stereotyping, and teacher education. *Teacher Education Quarterly, 24*(3), 5–19.

Solórzano, D. G., & Bernal, D. D. (2001). Examining transformational resistance through a critical race and LatCrit theory framework: Chicana and Chicano students in an urban context. *Urban Education, 36*(3), 308–342.

Solórzano, D. G., & Yosso, T. J. (2002). Critical race methodology: Counter-storytelling as an analytical framework for education research. *Qualitative Inquiry, 8*(1), 23–44.

Sotirovska, V., & Kelley, J. (2020). Anthropomorphic characters in children's literature: Windows, mirrors, or sliding glass doors to embodied immigrant experiences. *The Elementary School Journal, 121*(2), 337–355.

Souto-Manning, M. (2013). *Multicultural teaching in the early childhood classroom: Approaches, strategies, and tools, preschool–2nd grade.* Teachers College Press.

Souto-Manning, M., & Rabadi-Raol, A. (2018). (Re)centering quality in early childhood education: Toward intersectional justice for minoritized children. *Review of Research in Education, 42*(1), 203–225. https://doi.org/10.3102/0091732X18759550

Souto-Manning, M., & Turner, C. (2022). Early literacy research and theory on infants and toddlers: A strengths-based approach. In D. R. Meier (Ed.), *Critical issues in infant-toddler language development: Connecting theory to practice* (pp. 103–111). Routledge.

Souto-Manning, M., & Vasquez, V. M. (2011). *Practicing critical literacy in early childhood education: The how and the why.* Routledge.

Stacey, S. (2018). *Inquiry-based early learning environments: Creating, supporting, and collaborating.* Redleaf Press.

Stake, R. E. (1995). *The art of case study research.* Sage.

Sturdivant, T. D. (2020). *Developing while Black: An exploration of racial discourse found in the play of Black preschool girls* [Doctoral dissertation]. The University of Texas at San Antonio).

Sturdivant, T. D. (2021a). Complying and resisting: A qualitative metasynthesis of the race and gender discourses found in the play of young children. *Journal of Educational Studies and Multidisciplinary Approaches, 1*(2), 84–104.

Sturdivant, T. D. (2021b). Racial awareness and the politics in play: Preschoolers and racially diverse dolls in a US classroom. *International Journal of Early Childhood, 53*(2), 139–157.

Sturdivant, T. D. (2023). Going back to move forward. *Young Children, 78*(3), 50–57.

Sturdivant, T., & Alanís, I. (2019). Teaching through culture: One teacher's use of culturally relevant practices for African American preschoolers. *Journal for Multicultural Education, 13*(3), 203–214. https://doi.org/10.1108/JME-03-2019 -0019

Sturdivant, T. D., & Alanís, I. (2021). I'm gonna cook my baby in a pot: Young Black girls' racial preferences and play behavior. *Early Childhood Education Journal, 49*(3), 473–82.

Sullivan, P. (2022). Reading for liberation in early childhood—Promoting an anti-racist language and literacy curriculum. In D. R. Meier (Ed.), *Critical issues in infant-toddler language development—Connecting theory to practice* (pp. 54–61). Routledge.

Tager, M. (2022). *Anti-racist pedagogy in the early childhood classroom.* Lexington Books.

Takei, G. (2024). *My lost freedom* (M. Lee, Illus.). Crown Books.

Tarpley, N. A. (1998). *I love my hair!* (E. B. Lewis, Illus.). Little, Brown and Company.

Tatum, B. D. (2015). What is racism anyway? Understanding the basics of racism and prejudice. In S. M. McClure and C. A. Harris (Eds.), *Getting real about race: Hoodies, mascots, model minorities, and other conversations* (pp. 15–24.). Sage.

Tatum, B. D. (2017). "Why are all the Black kids still sitting together in the cafeteria?" and other conversations about race in the twenty-first century. *Liberal Education, 103*(3–4), 46–56.

Tatum, B. D. (2021). "What is racism anyway?": Understanding the basics of racism and prejudice. In S. M. McClure & C. A. Harris (Eds.), *Getting real about race* (3rd ed., pp. 17–26). SAGE.

Thomas, E. E. (2016). Stories "still" matter: Rethinking the role of diverse children's literature Today. *Language Arts, 94*(2), 112–119. https://www.jstor .org/stable/44809887

Valente, J. M., & Danforth, S. (2016). Disability studies in education: Storying our way to inclusion. *Occasional Paper Series, 2016*(36), 4–10.

Van Ausdale, D., & Feagin, J. R. (2002). *The first R: How children learn race and racism.* Rowman & Littlefield.

Vasquez, V. M. (2014). *Negotiating critical literacies with young children.* Routledge.

Vaughn, M., Parsons, S. A., & Gallagher, M. A. (2022). Challenging scripted curricula with adaptive teaching. *Educational Researcher, 51*(3), 186–196.

Venegas, E. M., & Guanzon, A. (2023). A planning tool for improving interactive read-alouds: Why and how. *The Reading Teacher, 77*(2), 207–216. https://doi .org/10.1002/trtr.2234

Vittrup, B. (2016). Early childhood teachers' approaches to multicultural education & perceived barriers to disseminating anti-bias messages. *Multicultural Education, 23*(3–4), 37–41.

Vygotsky, L. S. (1978). *Mind in society: The development of higher psychological processes.* Harvard University Press.

Whittaker, V. A., & Neville, H. A. (2010). Examining the relation between racial identity attitude clusters and psychological health outcomes in African American college students. *Journal of Black Psychology, 36*(4), 383–409. https://doi.org/10.1177/0095798409353757

Wild, N. R. (2023a). Picturebooks for social justice: Creating a classroom community grounded in identity, diversity, justice, and action. *Early Childhood Education Journal, 51*(4), 733–741. https://doi.org/10.1007/s10643-022-01342-1

Wild, N. R. (2023b). Teaching for social justice: A teacher researcher's journey and evolution. *The Reading Teacher, 77*(3), 360–370. https://doi.org/10.1002/trtr.2252

Winkler, E. N. (2009). Children are not colorblind: How young children learn race. *PACE, Practical Approaches for Continuing Education 3*(3), 1–8. https://inclusions.org/wp-content/uploads/2017/11/Children-are-Not-Colorblind.pdf

World of Words. Center of global literacies and literatures. (2020). *10 quick ways to analyze children's books for racism and sexism* (1980), published as a brochure by the Council on Interracial Books for Children (New York). Found at .https://wowlit.org/links/evaluating-global-literature/10-quick-ways-to-analyze-childrens-books-for-racism-and-sexism/

Wright, B. L. (2018). *The brilliance of Black boys: Cultivating school success in the early grades.* Teachers College Press.

Wright, B. L. (2021). What about the children: Teachers cultivating and nurturing the voice and agency of young children. In I. Alanís & I. U. Iruka (Eds.), *Advancing equity & embracing diversity in early childhood education,* 65–69. NAEYC.

Wright, T. S. (2019). Reading to learn from the start: The power of interactive read-alouds. *American Educator, 42*(4), 4–8.

Wynter-Hoyte, K., Braden, E., Boutte, G., Long, S., & Muller, M. (2022). Identifying anti-Blackness and committing to Pro-Blackness in early literacy pedagogy and research: A guide for child care settings, schools, teacher preparation programs, and researchers. *Journal of Early Childhood Literacy, 22*(4), 565–591.

Wynter-Hoyte, K., & Smith, M. (2020). "Hey, Black child. Do you know who you are?" Using African diaspora literacy to humanize blackness in early childhood education. *Journal of Literacy Research, 52*(4), 406–431.

Wynter-Hoyt, K., Thornton Adams, N., Smith, N, & Jones, K. (2021). A revolutionary love story in teacher education and early childhood education. Theory Into Practice, 60(3), 265–278.

Yu, M., Sintos, R., Wenyang, S., & Jungmin, K. (2004). Dissecting anti-Asian racism through a historical and transnational AsianCrit lens. *Sociological Inquiry, 94*(2), 330–350. https://doi.org/10.1111/soin.12572

Zirkel, S., & Johnson, T. (2016). Mirror, mirror on the wall: A critical examination of the conceptualization of the study of black racial identity in education. *Educational Researcher, 45*(5), 301–311. http://dx.doi.org/10.3102/0013189X16656938

# Online Resources

**Websites Related to Book Selection**

| | |
|---|---|
| Social Justice Books: A project of Teaching for Change, general information | https://socialjusticebooks.org/about/ |
| SJB Guide for selecting antibias children's books | https://socialjusticebooks.org/guide-for-selecting-anti-bias-childrens-books/ |
| SJB Early childhood antibias education book lists | https://socialjusticebooks.org/booklists/early-childhood/ |
| SJB 100 book lists by theme | https://socialjusticebooks.org/booklists/ |
| SJB Freedom Reads: Anti-Bias Book Talk videos "to strengthen parents' and teachers' anti-bias, anti-racism lens and their ability to critically analyze children's media." | https://socialjusticebooks.org/freedom-reads/ |
| Seattle Public Library list of race and social justice books for kids K–5 | https://www.spl.org/books-and-media/books-and-ebooks/staff-picks-for-kids/race-and-social-justice-books-for-kids-k-5 |
| We Are Teachers: 25+ inspiring social justice books for kids of all ages | https://www.weareteachers.com/books-about-social-justice/ |
| Little Parachutes: A collection of books that help children cope with worries, health issues, and new experiences. | https://www.littleparachutes.com/ |
| Children's Library Lady: Social justice picture books | https://childrenslibrarylady.com/social-justice-picture-books/ |
| Carnegie Library of Pittsburgh: Race and social justice books for kids | https://www.carnegielibrary.org/staff-picks/race-and-social-justice-books-for-kids/ |
| Children's Literature and Reading Special Interest Group, International Literacy Association: Notable Books for a Global Society list | http://clrsig.org/nbgs.html |

| Worlds of Words, Center of Global Literacies and Literature, University of Arizona: General information | http://wowlit.org/ |
|---|---|
| WOWLit: 10 quick ways to analyze children's books for racism and sexism | https://wowlit.org/links/evaluating-global-literature/10-quick-ways-to-analyze-childrens-books-for-racism-and-sexism/ |
| Conscious Kid: Children's books on race, racism, and resistance | https://www.theconsciouskid.org/antiracist-childrens-books |
| The National Center for Children's Illustrated Literature | https://www.nccil.org/ |
| The Center for the Study of Children's Literature at Simmons College | https://www.simmons.edu/academics/colleges-schools-departments/ifill/department-humanities/center-for-study-of-childrens-literature |
| The African American Children's Book Project | https://theafricanamericanchildrensbookproject.org/ |
| We Need Diverse Books | https://diversebooks.org/ |

## Resources for Learning Stories

| Supporting the Advancement of Learning Stories in America (SALSA) | https://salsa-global.org/ |
|---|---|
| Website by Tom Drummond: Drummond offers resources related to Learning Stories, initiating critical conversations with children, and structuring play-based learning. | https://tomdrummond.com/ |
| NAEYC Online Journal: *Voices of Practitioners*: This compilation of articles prompts conversations about the value of linking children's literacy-rich experiences across media types. | https://www.naeyc.org/resources/pubs/vop/dec2024 |
| Educational Leadership Project: Learning Stories | https://elp.co.nz/learning-stories/ |

## Author Websites and Blogs

| Jorge Argueta | https://jorgeargueta.com/ |
|---|---|
| Laurence Anholt | https://www.anholt.co.uk/ |
| Natasha Anastasia Tarpley | https://natashatarpleywrites.com/ |
| Dr. Kamshia Childs | https://drkchilds.com/ |
| Dr. Megan Pamela Ruth Madison | https://www.firstconversations.com/ |
| Dr. Toni D. Sturdivant | https://www.toniphd.com/ |

| | |
|---|---|
| Jerry Pinkney | https://www.justjerrypinkney.com/jerrys-life |
| Mo Willems | https://www.pigeonpresents.com/ |
| | https://www.nccil.org/artists/mo-willems |
| Christian Robinson | https://school.teachingbooks.net/tb.cgi?aid =20116 |
| | https://www.theartoffun.com/about/ |
| Nina Crews | https://ninacrews.com/ |
| René Colato Laínez Blog | http://www.renecolatolainez.net |

# Theory-Driven Approaches for the Integration of Culturally Relevant Children's Picture Books

| Theory-Driven Approaches | Strategies | Implementation |
|---|---|---|
| **Critical literacy circles (Freire, 1970; Lewison et al., 2002)** | Encourage children to question and analyze texts through a critical literacy lens. | • Ask open-ended questions that prompt students to think about power, identity, and representation.<br>• Use prompts such as *Who is represented in this book? Who is missing? Whose voice is the loudest?*<br>• Have students rewrite or re-tell portions of the text to include missing perspectives or challenge dominant narratives. |
| **Family storytelling integration (Moll et al., 1992, funds of knowledge; Esteban-Guitart & Moll, 2014, Esteban-Guitart, 2021, funds of identity)** | Engage families in co-creating and sharing stories that reflect their lived experiences and cultural traditions. | • Invite family members to share oral stories that align with themes in picture books.<br>• Create collaborative books where children and families contribute their own illustrations, dictations, and reflections in their home languages.<br>• Provide home-lending libraries for your community where families can freely borrow and return books. Ensure these are culturally relevant books that represent the languages in your community. |
| **Interactive read-alouds with social action (Harste, 2000; Souto-Manning, 2013)** | Extend discussions of picture books into real-world social action. | • Choose books that introduce themes of activism, fairness, and justice (e.g., *Separate Is Never Equal* (2014) by Duncan Tonatiuh).<br>• After reading, guide children in brainstorming small, developmentally appropriate actions (e.g., writing letters, making posters, creating class agreements about fairness).<br>• Connect book themes to local community issues and encourage class projects that involve families. |

*(continued)*

| Theory-Driven Approaches | Strategies | Implementation |
|---|---|---|
| **Multimodal response projects (Kress, 2010, multimodality theory)** | Allow children to respond to literature through multiple forms of expression (art, music, drama, digital media). | • Encourage children to create storyboards, podcasts, or digital storytelling projects based on culturally relevant books.<br>• Offer materials for artistic responses such as painting, sculpting, or collaging their interpretations.<br>• Use drama-based pedagogy to reenact and problem-solve scenarios from the stories. |
| **Dual-language and translanguaging approaches (Arreguín-Anderson & Alanís, 2019; García & Wei, 2014)** | Incorporate bilingual books and support children in using multiple languages to discuss and engage with literature (see Chapter 4 of this text). | • Select bilingual picture books that affirm students' linguistic identities.<br>• Encourage translanguaging during book discussions, allowing students to use their full linguistic repertoire.<br>• Invite multilingual family members to read and discuss books in their home languages. |
| **Culturally sustaining book selection (Paris & Alim, 2017, culturally sustaining pedagogy)** | Move beyond diverse books to texts that actively sustain and celebrate students' cultural practices. | • Include contemporary stories alongside historical narratives to validate students' current realities.<br>• Let children and families recommend books that reflect their experiences and cultures. |
| **Bookmaking as identity affirmation (Dyson, 2003; Vasquez, 2014)** | Encourage children to co-create books that reflect their lived experiences. | • Support children in making picture books about their families, traditions, or social justice topics they care about.<br>• Allow students to dictate, write, or illustrate their own culturally relevant stories.<br>• Display and share student-created books to validate their identities and voices. |
| **Cross-cultural dialogues with literature (Bishop, 1990, windows, mirrors, and sliding glass doors)** | Use literature as a bridge for cross-cultural discussions among students and families. | • Pair students with different cultural backgrounds to discuss picture books and personal connections.<br>• Facilitate intergenerational book clubs where parents, grandparents, and children discuss social justice themes together.<br>• Use books as "mirrors" (reflecting students' identities) and "windows" (offering perspectives on others' experiences) |

# Children's Books on Equity, Kindness, and Belonging, With Discussion Prompts

## Children's Books About Kindness and Empathy

| | |
|---|---|
| *Be Kind*—Pat Zietlow Miller (2018). A gentle story about small acts of kindness and their big impact. | What are some small ways we can show kindness every day?<br><br>How does kindness make people feel? |
| *Each Kindness*—Jacqueline Woodson (2012). Explores missed opportunities for kindness and the power of compassion. | How do you think Maya felt when no one wanted to be her friend?<br><br>Why is it important to be kind, even when no one is watching? |
| *I Walk With Vanessa*—Kerascoët (2018). A wordless book about standing up against bullying through kindness. | How did Vanessa feel when she was bullied?<br><br>What are some ways you can stand up for someone who is being treated unfairly? |
| *Strictly No Elephants*—Lisa Mantchev (2015). Celebrates inclusion and friendship through an imaginative story about a boy and his pet elephant. | Have you ever felt left out? How did it make you feel?<br><br>Why is it important to include everyone, even if they are different from us? |
| *A Little Spot of Kindness*—Diane Alber (2019). Examples of how everyone can spread kindness in everyday interactions. | What are some places you can show kindness?<br><br>How does it feel when someone is kind to you?<br><br>How does it feel when you are kind to someone else? |
| *A Sick Day for Amos McGee*—Philip C. Stead (2010). A heartwarming story about a zookeeper's kindness to animals and their kindness in return. | How did Amos show kindness to the animals?<br><br>How did the animals show kindness in return? |
| *Two Nests*—Laurence Anholt (2013). Shows how family separations can be confusing and unsettling. It reassures children that family life can continue happily even if parents are living apart. | How does baby bird feel about having to fly between two nests? What could you say to baby bird to make him feel better?<br><br>How do Betty and Paul reassure baby bird? |

## Children's Picture Books about Equity, Inclusion, and Diversity

| | |
|---|---|
| *All Are Welcome*—Alexandra Penfold (2018). Shows a diverse classroom where everyone belongs. | What does it mean to make people feel welcome? How can we make sure everyone in our school or community feels included? |
| *The Proudest Blue*—Ibtihaj Muhammad (2019). A story of resilience and pride in identity, focusing on a girl's first day wearing a hijab. | What does the hijab mean to Faizah and Asiya? Why is it important to be proud of who we are? |
| *We're All Wonders*—R. J. Palacio (2017). Celebrates kindness, belonging, and friendship—teaching empathy for those who look different. | How do you think Auggie feels when people stare at him? What can we do to make sure everyone feels accepted? |
| *Say My Name*—Joanna Ho (2023). Explores cultural identity and embracing one's unique name. | Why did Unhei feel nervous about her name? How can we show respect for names that are different from our own? |
| *Intersection Allies: We Make Room for All*—Chelsea Johnson, LaToya Council, and Carolyn Choi (2019). A simple introduction to intersectionality for young readers. | What does it mean to be an ally? How can we help friends who are treated unfairly? |

## Children's Picture Books on Justice & Standing Up for Others

| | |
|---|---|
| *Say Something*—Peter H. Reynolds (2019). Encourages kids to speak up against injustice and use their voices for good. | What are some ways we can use our voices to help others? Have you ever seen something unfair? What could you do in that situation? |
| *Change Sings*—Amanda Gorman (2021). A poetic call to action about making a difference, illustrated by Loren Long. | What does "change" mean in this story? How can kids help change the world? |
| *Sometimes People March*—Tessa Allen (2020). Explains protests and activism in an accessible way for young children. | Why do people march? What are some peaceful ways people can stand up for what is right? |
| *Peaceful Fights for Equal Rights*—Rob Sanders (2018). A powerful ABC book about activism and standing up for what is right. | What are some ways to speak up for justice? How can art, music, or writing help make the world better? |
| *One Love*—Cedella Marley (2011). Based on Bob Marley's song, this book spreads a message of unity and love. | What does "One Love" mean? How can we spread love in our families, schools, and communities? |

# List of Children's Literature Cited

Ada, A. F. (2002). *I love Saturdays y domingos* (E. Savadier, Illus.). Atheneum.

Agna, G. (2024). *Finding home: Words from kids seeking sanctuary* (S. Rotner, Illus.). Clarion Books.

Anholt, L. (2013). *Two nests.* (J. Coplestone, Illus.). Frances Lincoln Children's Books.

Argueta, J. (2006). *Talking with Mother Earth/Hablando con madre tierra* (L. Perez, Illus.). Groundwood Books.

Argueta, J. (2013). *Xochitl and the Flowers/Xóchitl, la niña de las flores* (C. Angel, Illus.). Lee & Low Books.

Argueta, J. (2007). *A movie in my pillow/Una película en mi almohada* (E. Gómez, illus.). Children's Book Press.

Argueta, J. (2007). *Alfredito flies home/Alfredito regresa volando a su casa* (L. Garay, Illus). Groundwood Books.

Argueta, J. (2009). *Sopa de frijoles/Bean soup* (R. Yockteng, Illus.). Groundwood Books.

Argueta, J. (2016). *Somos como las nubes/We are like the clouds* (A. Ruano, Illus.). Groundwood Books.

Argueta, J. T. (2017). *Agua, agüita/Water, little water* (F. U. Alcántara, Illus.). Arte Público Press.

Banker, A. (2020). *I am Brown* (S. Prabhat, Illus.). Lantana Publishing.

Childs, K. R. (2024). *I am more than my name* (B. James, Illus.). EdWhys Publishing.

Colato Laínez, R. (2009). *René has two last names/René tiene dos apellidos.* (F. Graullera Ramírez, Illus.). Arte Público Press.

Colato Laínez, R. (2010). *The tooth fairy meets El Ratón Pérez* (T. Lintern, Illus.). Tricycle Press.

Colato Laínez, R. (2015). *Waiting for papá/Esperando a papá* (A. Accardo, Illus.). Arte Público Press.

Colato Laínez, R. (2016). *Mamá the Alien/Mamá la extraterrestre* (L. Lacámara, Illus.). Children's Books Press.

Cole, J. B., & LaTeef, N. (2021). *African proverbs for all ages* (N. LaTeef, Illus.). Roaring Book Press.

de la Peña, M. (2018). *Carmela full of wishes* (C. Robinson, Illus.). G.P. Putnam's Sons.

Dennis, E. (2022). *The boy from Mexico: An immigration story of bravery and determination.* Dragonfruit.

Devenny, J. (2021). *Race cars: A children's book about white privilege*. Frances Lincoln Children's Books.

Easton, E. (2018). *Enough! 20+ protesters who changed America* (Z. Chen, Illus.). Penguin Random House.

Evans, S. W. (2012). *We march*. Roaring Press.

Farrell, K. (2020). *V is for voting* (C. Kuhwald, Illus.). Henry Holt.

Ho, J. (2023). *Say my name* (K. Le, Illus.). HarperCollins.

Iyengar, M. M. (2009). *Tan to tamarind: Poems about the color brown* (J. Akib, Illus.). Children's Books Press.

Keats, E. J. (1962). *The snowy day*. Viking Books.

Lyons, K. S. (2019). *Going down home with daddy* (D. Minter, Illus.). Peachtree Publishing

Lyons, K. S. (2019). *Sing a song: How "Lift Every Voice and Sing" inspired generations* (K. Mallet, Illus.). Nancy Paulsen Books.

Madison, M., & Ralli, J. (2021). *Our skin: A first conversation about race.* (I. Roxas, Illus.). Rise.

Madison, M., & Ralli, J. (2024). *We care* (S, Miller, Illus). Rise.

Manushkin, F. (2018). *Happy in our skin* (L. Tobia, Illus.). Candlewick Press.

Medina, J. (1999). *My name is Jorge on both sides of the river: Poems in English and Spanish* (F. Vanden Broeck, Illus.). Wordsong/Boyds Mills Press.

Medina, M. (2015). *Mango, Abuela, and me.* (A. Dominguez, Illus.). Children's Books Press.

Meltzer, B. (2015). *I am Jackie Robinson* (C. Eliopoulos, Illus.). Rocky Pond Books.

Méndez, Y. S. (2019). *¿De dónde eres?* (J. Kim, Illus.). HarperCollins

Morales, A. (2021). *Areli is a dreamer* (L. Uribe, Illus.). Random House Studio.

Morales, Y. (2015). *Niño wrestles the world*. Roaring Brook Press.

Morales, Y. (2018). *Dreamers/Soñadores*. Neal Porter Books.

Odeh, M. (2024). *A map for Falasteen* (A. Betawi, Illus.). Henry Holt.

Paul, M. (2020). *Speak up* (E. Glenn, Illus.). Clarion Books.

Perry, L. (2016). *Skin like mine* (B. Jackson, Illus.). G Publishing.

Pimentel, A. B. (2020). *All the way to the top: How one girl's fight for Americans with disabilities changed everything* (N. H. Ali, Illus.). Sourcebooks.

Robinson, C. (2019). *another*. Atheneum Books.

Rose, T. (2019). *M is for melanin*. Little Bee Books.

Takei, G. (2024). *My lost freedom* (M. Lee, Illus.). Crown Books.

Tarpley, N. A. (1998). *I love my hair!* (E. B. Lewis, Illus.). Little, Brown and Company.

# Family Story Retelling Invitation (*Invitación Para Volver a Contar la Historia en Familia*)

Dear Families,

We have been reading the story [Book Title] in class. Now, we invite you to retell the story at home with your child. Use any of the strategies below.

Queridas familias, en clase hemos leído el cuento [Título del libro]. Ahora les invitamos a volver a contar la historia en casa con su hijo/a. Use cualquiera de las estrategias que aparecen a continuación:

| | | | |
|---|---|---|---|
| Strategy 1 | Draw or paint a favorite part of the story. | Estrategia 1 | Dibujar o pintar su parte favorita de la historia. |
| Strategy 2 | Act it out with toys, puppets, or costumes. | Estrategia 2 | Representarla con juguetes, títeres o disfraces. |
| Strategy 3 | Tell the story in Spanish, English, or both. | Estrategia 3 | Contar la historia en español, inglés o en los dos idiomas. |
| Strategy 4 | Invent a new ending or add a new character. | Estrategia 4 | Inventar un nuevo final o agregar un nuevo personaje. |
| Strategy 5 | Sing, dance, or make a short video. | Estrategia 5 | Cantar, bailar o hacer un pequeño video. |

**Family Retelling Space (Write, draw, or add ideas)**
**Espacio para volver a contar la historia en familia (Escriba, dibuje o agregue ideas)**

No one way is "correct." Every family's story is valuable.

No existe una sola manera "correcta." Cada historia de cada familia es valiosa.

Please return your child's project by [Date].

Por favor entregue el proyecto de su hijo/a antes del [Fecha].

Thank you! / ¡Gracias!

# Index

# About the Authors and Contributors

**Isauro M. Escamilla** is assistant professor of elementary education at San Francisco State University. Born and raised in Veracruz, Mexico, Isauro taught preschool for many years in the San Francisco Unified School District. Isauro specialized in bilingual education and has a special interest in bilingual children's literature, culturally responsive education, and supportive relationships with families and communities. Isauro also has extensive experience with inquiry groups and professional learning communities, as well as experience in international research in Japan, Mexico, Palestine, and Aotearoa/New Zealand.

**Iliana Alanís** is a professor of early childhood and elementary education within the Department of Interdisciplinary Learning and Teaching at The University of Texas at San Antonio. Iliana's research and teaching interests focus on the academic success of young Latinx children in dual language classrooms, language policy, and Latina scholars in academia. Iliana is especially interested in forms of teaching that promote native language development and its correlation to second-language acquisition. She focuses on teaching practices in early childhood classrooms and the effect of quality schooling on language minority children in dual language programs. Born and raised in the Rio Grande Valley of Texas, Iliana is deeply committed to the multilingual development and growth of young children on both sides of the Rio Grande border.

**Daniel Meier** is professor of elementary education at San Francisco State University, and teaches multiple subject credential candidates, MA students in early childhood education, and doctoral students in educational leadership. His teaching and scholarship focus on children's early language and literacy development, qualitative research, teacher inquiry, narrative inquiry and memoir, and international education. Daniel has also worked with teachers for many years in professional learning communities and inquiry groups, as well as conducting research and working with teachers in Japan, the United Kingdom, Mexico, and Palestine.

## ABOUT THE CONTRIBUTORS

*Laura Cardona Berrio* is a former elementary teacher with over 10 years of experience in elementary education, in nontraditional educational settings, and at the university level in Colombia. She taught drama and dance as artistic expressions to support and empower children from financially disadvantaged backgrounds. She is a doctoral candidate in the Department of Interdisciplinary Learning and Teaching at the University of Texas at San Antonio. Her area of research focuses on bilingual education, culturally sustaining biliteracy pedagogical practices, the effective teaching practices of Latina inservice teachers, and social justice issues within early childhood settings. Through a culturally sustaining pedagogies framework, Laura seeks to improve the educational experiences of culturally and linguistically diverse young children.

*Maria Leija* is a former elementary teacher who taught for 6 years in Idaho. During that time, she helped develop and implement an 80/20 two-way bilingual immersion program, was a Spanish dual language teacher, and taught in the mainstream class while supporting the academic language development of her emerging bilingual students. Her research focuses on elementary Latinx preservice and inservice teachers' pedagogical practices in Spanish/English bilingual classrooms. Leija utilizes Latino critical race theory to examine classroom discourse and pedagogical practices. She has examined and published the use of children's literature for teaching social studies and language arts by analyzing themes such as immigration, gender, and Latinx community cultural practices.

*Toni D. Sturdivant* has taught Head Start in San Antonio ISD, prekindergarten as a master teacher for the City of San Antonio's Pre-K 4 SA initiative, and kindergarten for an online public school. Dr. Sturdivant has served as a trainer for early childhood teachers as a professional learning specialist, where she coached and mentored educators and created and facilitated engaging and interactive workshops. She worked as an assistant professor of early childhood education at Texas A&M University–Commerce, teaching preservice teachers in the College of Education and Human Services, and has published numerous research articles. Her research focuses on positive identity development in young children through an intersectional lens. Her teaching centers on equity, social justice, and cultural relevance paired with high-quality interactions in a social constructivist environment.

***Patricia Sullivan*** holds an MA in early childhood education and an EdD in educational leadership. She is the owner and director of Baby Steps, a home-based childcare program in San Francisco. Pat is a veteran early childhood educator, highly experienced with inquiry, reflection, antiracist education, and language and literacy teaching. Pat is a passionate advocate for equity and social justice in early childhood education, and her research publications have focused on reconceptualizing education for all children and families, nature education, narrative inquiry, and critical literacy.